Preface

Many books have been written by politicians, entertainers, news people and talk show hosts. These books, though informative and well written, tend to express the opinions of the well educated upper class folks limited in their practical experience of life in the Ghetto or Barrio. Their opinions are not necessarily a complete and comprehensive perspective of those of us not of the country club set.

However, this book written by a guy born in East Los Angeles and raised as a minority of Mexican heritage, barely made it out of High School. My thoughts and opinions were basically formed by my family, friends, the media, and the educational system. Living in the stereotypical era of the fifties, I was thoroughly convinced I was inferior to the white man. A man, who automatically assumed he was superior.
As a retired Geezer, I felt compelled to share a few of my experiences and thoughts in what I've learned in my seventy plus years concerning racism and the people who practice it. I was inspired by the obvious rash of racism that has surfaced with the coming of Obama. I believe his presence has exposed those of us still harboring antiquated, yet strong, racist feelings.

Prejudice folks generally do not see themselves as racist – and when caught in a racial faux pas publically defend themselves with, "I am not a racist!" I've always found this statement silly – Hell, we're all racists to some degree! Whether it's simply giggling over an ethnic joke at someone's expense, or joining a radical racist group. So with said, and because of my limited education, please excuse the bad English, poor grammar, and typos that follow.

Contents

A history of the calculated and systematic control of minorities

An Obtuse View of Racism in America

By
Albert A. Obregon

With the coming of Obama,

And his promise of change, we once again see the faces of the young and old alike brightened with the "Audacity of Hope". And with this promise of change, we also see the old and established look at this change with fear. This country is once again confronted with the growing pains of a character and complexion adjustment.

This excerpt is taken from an article written tongue-in-cheek in 2008 by Rosa Brooks, entitled: **The 'real' America, really.**

Behind the anger and the us-versus them rhetoric we've seen at recent McCain-Palin rallies, with a palpable sense of dislocation and anxiety: The anxiety of those who feel that things are slipping away from them, that the world is changing too quickly and too uncomfortably. Change has come fast - and change hurts.

But that's how it's always been. Our culture was built by immigrants and shaped by wars, social upheavals, economic crises and further rounds of immigration, each time from places that seemed "foreign" to those who had already settled in. Each round of changes was painful to those used to the temporary status quo - but each round of change also gave us a richer stronger nation.

That's the real America: A land of change and perpetual renewal.

Let's not stand for it!

Rosa Brooks
L.A. Times Columnist

Part One

RACE AND ITS ORIGIN

IN THE BEGINNING, and a long, long time ago, some smart guys (Anthropologists) noticed a big difference between some of the People. (Homo sapiens) Like for instance the shape and color of their hair, skin, and eyes - Or simply the differences in their physical structure.

Because of these differences, it was decided to classify the people into separate groups. Now just how many of these groups was another thing! The Anthropologists were asked to submit lists as to how many different groups they thought we should have.

These submitted lists which varied in numbers from 2 to 60 were both too little and too many. It was then decided to simply separate these people based primarily on their skin color narrowing the list down to three groups: Caucasoid, Negroid, and Mongoloid. This took in the geographic areas of Europe, Africa, and Asia.

Negroid (Africa) Negro, a word derived from the Spanish and Portuguese for black – Adopted into English in the 16th century referring to dark skinned people of Africa.

Caucasoid (Europe) Caucasian, a term used by early anthropologists in referring to light-skinned people of Europe and surrounding areas - People originating from Caucasia.

Mongoloid (East Asian region of Mongolia) A racial group of people stemming from East and South-East Asia – and the Native Americans of North and South America. (Injuns)

With the problem settled and the champagne flowing, someone broke up the party by mentioning the Aborigines of Australia and how they were unique in physical appearances - some having dark skin similar to Africans, and others radically different with blond hair like the Norsemen. Unable to fit them in a Negroid, Caucasoid, or Mongoloid mold, they created a new category for the Australians called "Australoid." - Clever, huh?

These four groups of people are listed as… "RACE"

The dictionary defines race as: Family – Tribe - Lineage – Individuals sprung from a common stock

Primarily with the world pretty well separated geographically, these four racial groups were content to live with their own kind. But necessity, along with brave and daring hearts, caused some with restless feet to venture on to explore other lands. As these migrating newcomers settled in lands inhabited by people of different cultures and colors, they were received as unusual and treated in a negative manner – forcing them to assimilate in clustered groups.

As world migration increased, and with propagation in full swing, the big mix was on. With Nature taking its natural course, and having no regard for color, the four major races diversified into a mix of odd looking colors and shapes. And In time these spin-offs of various hues continued to multiply expanding further the racial diversity to numbers no longer calculable, making the original big four of Negroid, Caucasian, Mongoloid, and Australoid almost obsolete.

Besides the different shape and color of people, we also ignore the cultural differences deserving of their own identity - Such as the Inuit (Eskimo) of the Artic, and the jungle natives of the Amazon in South America. And let us not forget the dissimilarity in cultures between the Indians of the Far East, and the natives of the Western Hemisphere who were tagged "Indian" by an Italian explorer who mistakenly thought he landed in India.

When this misguided explorer opened the doors to the West, it invited Europeans and the likes to migrate to the new world in droves. Whether inherent or culturally induced, these light skinned immigrants automatically considered themselves to be of a higher level of being. When this mind set of superiority was bought over and established as fact, it created the bigotry and racism that exists today.

Like the immigration of today involving Hispanics coming here to seek work and a better life, these European Caucasians of old did the same thing. They came here illegally, without authority or permission of the native inhabitants. They too wanted to grab a piece of the hope and opportunity that this land had to offer. The big difference was the White Anglos didn't come here with the intentions of working with or serving the natives of this land, they came here with a much bigger vision - ONE OF PERSONAL GAIN - To conquer and rule!

With their white superiority established, these European aliens, used and abused the darker skinned natives for their own purpose. Unfortunately for the Redskins, this abusive treatment included a series of white mans broken treaties lasting hundreds of years. This is where we learned that the **"White man speaks with forked tongue."** The native Indians were eventually reduced to living in designated reservations through out the states as wards of the government.

4

The fact that most racial lines have been blurred beyond recognition has caused the powers that be in this country to ignore the original names of Caucasoid, Negroid, Mongoloid, and Australoid and divide this new multi-hued society into two major groups – **"Whites,"** in one group and all the rest in the other. The other being **"People of Color"** or more commonly known as **"Minority"**.

The term **"People of Color"** is a favorite among Whites in reference to non-whites. - Especially when it comes to African Americans. At one time African Americans were called Negros or Colored People. But now with political correctness in order, they're no longer called colored people; they're called People of Color. Makes sense, huh?

The term minority does not necessarily mean a group of a lesser amount. In reality it has become a code word for less qualified. A minority, in order to exist somewhat comfortably in this society, will generally go along with the program by accepting his lower status.

We are constantly reminded that this nation is a melting pot of immigrants - a plethora of colors and cultures. Yet for some reason, and after all these years, there are some of a lighter hue, who reject the melting pot honestly believing they are a cut above minorities and therefore resist the urge to merge?

These elite Whites have always enjoyed their edge in the competition for the bigger piece of the pie. That's one of the reasons Whites in power have drawn a strong line separating Whites from the rest of the herd. In the old days if a white person was found to have one drop of black blood in him, regardless of his ancestry or origin, he was kicked out of the select group of "White" and banished forever to the depths of Blackville.

The offspring's of Whites that co-mingled with native Indians were called half-breeds and ostracized from both races - Same with Mexicans who are a mixture of Indian and Spanish blood. (Mestizos) They too, were not welcome by either the Spanish or the Indians.

In the United States "People of Color" are usually pigeon-holed into separate colors representative of their geographical origin; like African Americans are Black, Hispanics/Latinos are Brown, Asians are Yellow, and Native Americans are Red. Hey! What about those white folks? Don't they have an ethnicity? How come they're not called Caucasians, Anglos, Arians, or even European immigrants, huh??? Have all those names been exchanged for the simple sanitary title of "White?" And why is this precious title of white, which is unrepresentative of any ethnicity or geographical area, reserved solely for the Gringos?

As you look at the various values in each race, you'll find quite a mixture. There are light skinned whites and dark skinned Whites -same as Asians, Indians, and Blacks. You've probably, in your walk of life, run across some Blacks, Latinos, and Asians that have a lighter skin tone than some Whites. Especially some Asians with their beautiful ivory and alabaster skin color.

Then there's the beauty of the golden tan which minorities naturally sport - which in this country is treated as a negative - Unless the tan is artificially applied on a white person. Like fer instance guys like Cary Grant and George Hamilton who managed to keep an unnaturally looking golden tan most of their hay-day – maybe that's why there's a tanning salon on every street corner in Beverly Hills.

What is also important in this country is the value of ones skin color. As a Mexican, I would consider myself as one with a lighter skin. I remember as a kid hearing one of my sisters cry because she was not allowed to swim in the public swimming pool. Yet my lighter skinned sister, who was with her, was allowed in the pool anytime.

In thumbing through Webster's dictionary I was surprised to find such an array of varied definitions of how color relates to character. Let's see how radically **"different"** these colors are.

WHITE

The dictionary defines white as, **free from spot or blemish - marked by upright fairness – Innocent - free from moral impurity - free from color** (reduced pigmentation in the skin) Webster's definition pertaining to the characteristics of White people is quite positive. I found it interesting in the frequent use of the word "FREE." And I wonder what "free from color" would really look like?

After Webster's lengthy definition of **"White"** as a good and clean thing, he goes on to single out **"White"** as **"DIFFERENT"** from the rest of the herd - A group which includes the people of **black, brown, yellow or red skin.** Why would Webster draw such a distinct separation between Whites and the rest of the people?

This difference that Webster refers to, whether knowingly or unknowingly, subtle or blatant in its association with race, though kind and favorable to Whites, is rather brutal in defining those that are considered People of Color. Where did this Webster guy get his descriptive information defining racial character that historically would have such a lasting and damaging affect on those of color?

8

A brutal look at Minorities/People of Color

BLACK

(African American)

Webster defines Black as very dark in color or relating to a group or race characterized by dark pigmentation – of or relating to the Negro race. In contrast to his definition of "Whites," Webster then becomes somewhat negative as he defines black characteristics as – **dirty soiled – thoroughly sinister or evil – wicked**. These are just a few negatives in a long list of definitions relating to Black.

BROWN

(Mexicans/Latinos)

The color brown is defined as of the color brown - the mixture of the various shades and hues that create the color brown - a brown skinned person. Other than a brief description of the color brown nothing is suggested either positive or negative of the character of Brown People. *(Honest, there was no mention of laziness or of being shiftless with a tendency to migrate)*

9

YELLOW

(Asians)

However the color yellow, beside defined as having a yellow or light brown complexion, **means cowardly and mean.** Again, we have a color that defines racial characteristics negatively. Most would admit that Yellow, as a character description, represents cowardous. *(He has a yellow streak down his back)* - Like the captain of the movie "The Cain Mutiny, starring Humphrey Bogart, who is labeled "Ol' Yellow Stain" for retreating under fire in fear of artillery shells.

RED

(Indians)

Other than a description of the color red, no characteristics of red people are mentioned. However, under the word **red-skin,** a short two line description: American Indian, usu. **taken to be offensive.**

When the White man invaded the land of the Redskin, he not only conquered them, he enslaved them. He rationalized his behavior, by creating an undesirable image of the Redman. One undesirable image that comes to mind, **"The only good Indian is a dead Indian."**

It's apparent, with the dictionary's definition of the races, that white is the color of choice. So with that said, is it any wonder why..."**Light skinned immigrants from Europe prefer the title of White as opposed to the ethnic sounding names of European or Anglo.**"

Most would agree that Webster's definition of colors in representing race is pretty well in the mind set of this nation. I personally have never really seen a pure white person or a person that was truly black - nor have I ever seen a red or yellow person. However, I have seen people made up of all the imaginable hues of flesh color - from the darkest umbers to the lightest beiges. It's like we're all of the same flesh tone –Only different values!

A Diverse Blend of Flesh

Looking at this blended grey strip of values, I'm still confused as to why "We" minorities (actually a majority) allow ourselves to be so strongly segregated from the "Whites." (Actually, a minority when compared to the rest of us)

White, in the United States is not just a color defining a race, it is an elite social status enjoyed by the fair haired primarily of European immigrants. With this feeling of superiority over people considered minorities, Whites historically have enjoyed the perks and seating arrangement of riding first class. Adding to the misconception of white superiority is the general subservient attitude of most minorities who have reluctantly adopted their negative stereotypical image and are now accustomed to riding coach.

Most minorities, if asked, will tell you of the many negative racial encounters they've experienced in their lifetime on a regular daily basis. Whites, on the other hand, will sympathetically complain of an Anglo acquaintance of theirs who's been temporarily affected negatively by this bad and unfair affirmative action.

Speaking of affirmative action, in early two-thousand I wrote a letter on the subject which was published in the Los Angeles Daily News. This letter was inspired by a single white female complaining of how "affirmative action" had a negative effect on her college enrollment. I was surprised that this subject, which customarily never catches the president's ear, would cause George W. Bush to speak up on her behalf. He denounced affirmative action for discriminating against this white girl because of the color of her skin.

Regarding the president's intervention on this white girl's plight for equality, I wrote a letter in early 2000 to the Los Angeles Daily News which was published in the "Opinion Section."

Inequities of prejudice

Affirmative action is causing a few irate whites to experience once in their lives what all minorities put up with for most of theirs. Air-wave prattle on affirmative action is pretty well-divided along color lines. Recent complaints from these discriminated whites are but a whisper compared with the continued scream of discontented minorities locked in a state of rejection.

Yet, this whisper has caught the president's ear long enough for him to voice his disapproval of affirmative action and its negative effect on whites because of their skin color. Some whites will never know or understand the subtle and sometimes blatant inequities of prejudice.

— Albert Obregon
Sunland

Humm...how awful, a person actually treated unfairly because of the color of their skin.

It's understandable why Whites, who claim a higher level of existence, are not in favor of affirmative action, or for that matter, any other changes that would level the playing field to their disadvantage.

The jury is still out in some cases as to who qualifies as White. The vagueness of it all creates somewhat of a dilemma for the lighter skinned minorities. A good number of these lighter hued individuals, vying for the advantages and perks of the Whites, have managed to sneak into first class by passing themselves off as White.

One good example that comes to mind is of a young singer of the seventies by the name of Vicky Carr. A stage hand (Mexican guy) on the "Tonight show," met Vicky backstage and out of curiosity came right out and asked her if she was a Mexican. She admitted she was, and that her real name was Cardenas. She further added that she used the name of Carr to help her career. She is now a world renowned singer who records in both English and Spanish.

History has proven that Whites in most cases, although a minority, usually end up running things. This is due to the fact that minorities are led to believe that whites are smarter and better people. But as of late, with the changing face of the country, the theory that whites are indeed superior has kinda lost much of its punch.

The status of today's racial strife between whites and minorities has come a long way from the days of old, but still is a far cry from where we should be. What we definitely need is another option of race - Perhaps a common race composed of citizens not considered eligible for the exclusive white club. You know, like "People of Color," who by shear numbers would then be the majority race – and no longer be considered minorities!

Not caring for the title "People of Color," and somewhat of an artist, I did a little experimenting to see what would happen if I mixed the colors representative of the races black, brown, yellow, and red. I ended up coming up with a nice golden color. I asked myself, why we minorities can't be referred to as "Gold?" Now that's a name we can all live with. And even Webster likes it! He has a favorable definition for Gold: *"A symbol of what is valuable or much prized."*

So we simply take all the populace considered People of color, or those of a minority group, and form a new race called "Gold." This would eliminate the negative labels of **Minority or People of color -** bringing us to a racial status of two classes, "White and Gold" Perhaps with this change, the power which has solely belonged to the white ruling class, would then switch from the minority white race to the greater majority of the **"Gold Race."**

Could you imagine all the changes that would take place! The nation's politics, business, and media operations that have historically been operated and enjoyed by a minority of whites would then be controlled by this new majority of "Golden People." The nation's problems would then be viewed, and considered by a majority of the people - hopefully ridding us of the racial problems that have plagued this nation for so long.

Let's go back to the beginning and see how it was when the first immigrant first set foot on this land.

Part Two

MIGRATION

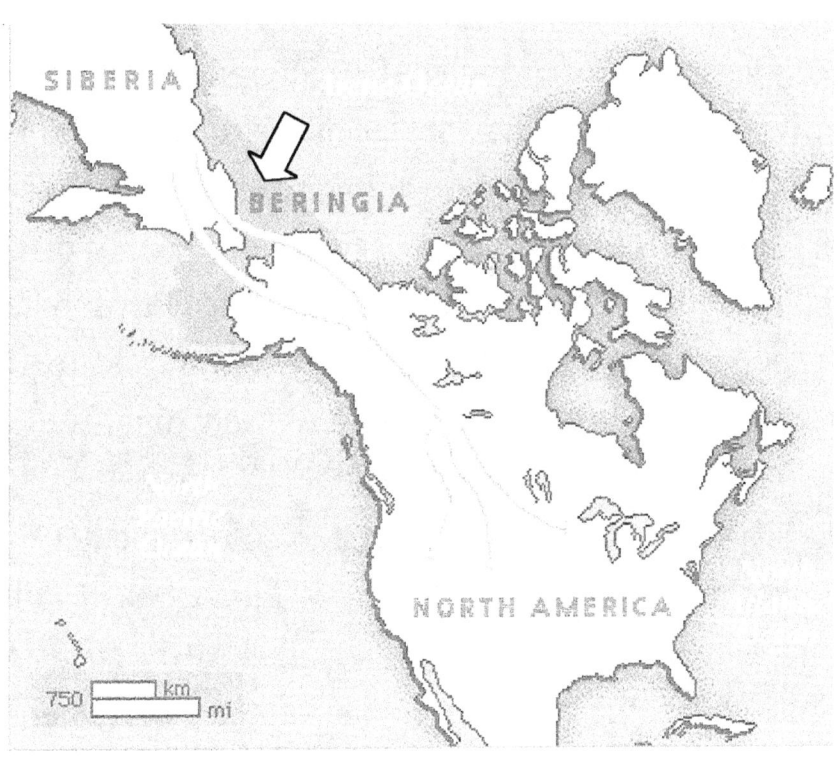

It's been estimated that 10 to 25 thousand years ago the first visitors to North America walked across the Beringia Land Bridge that spanned Asia and Alaska. These first inhabitants of the Americas were believed to be the ancestors of our Native American Indians.

This was just the beginning - what followed, whether by choice or necessity, was a constant flow of migrants of various cultures either wanting refuge or simply seeking a better life. This can either be a positive or a negative thing depending on the circumstance of the people on the receiving end of the influx – **AND,** the color of their skin.

The largest and most popular of all migration movements, involving the United States, was the Europeans who fled the oppression of their homeland in search of a better life. The Europeans did find a better life in this land of plenty, but only at the expense of the Natives. The native Indians were soon the new oppressed as they were forced to give up their way of life for the benefit of the white invaders.

This is a good example of when skin color, whether light or dark, can be a big factor in ones future. Now today, with the influx of darker skins infiltrating the "Whitelands," the rules of old do not necessarily pertain to the immigration problems of today. In April of 08, a letter was published in a Los Angeles newspaper written by a disgruntled citizen complaining of the modern day influx of Latino immigrants. The letter stated: *"If you come here, expect to work and assimilate into our society, not the other way around, and we will expect you to abide by our laws."*

18

After taking a minute to digest the words of the letter, so as to truly understand its meaning, I wondered if the writer's ancestors in coming to this country were of the same mind-set when they illegally stepped off the Mayflower onto Plymouth Rock." I don't think so!

This mass European migration to this new land came about with the discovery of the new world in 1492 by Christobal Colon. (Spanish for Christopher Columbus) The idea that the Vikings and Norsemen had founded Canada a thousand years earlier was completely ignored.

This Christobal guy, with three ships and a crew of about ninety guys furnished by King Ferdinand and Queen Isabella of Spain, is credited with discovering this land called the Americas. As an incentive to find the new land, a bonus, of $10,000 a year pension was offered by the King and Queen to the first man to lay eyes on the new world.

Contrary to the belief that Columbus was the first man to see land, a crewman aboard the "Pinta" by the name of Juan Rodriguez Bermejo claims he was the first one to see land. While on lookout in the early morning of October 12, 1492 this Juan guy by the first light of day, spotted land and yelled, "Tierra" – meaning land in English. But lo and behold, this Christobal guy told the queen that he had seen land the night before, therefore claiming the reward for himself. (Sure!!!)

When Christobal Colon first landed in the Bahamas, and thinking he was on an island in the Indies, named the locals "Indios" – Spanish for Indian. Hence, all natives indigenous to what we now know as the Americas would be, from that moment on, referred to as Indians.

Columbus dazzling the natives with shiny stuff

So, with the "Indios" looking on, Colon claimed the new land for Spain, naming it San Salvador. In further exploration, when Colon discovered Cuba and Hispaniola, he thought it was China.

The Native "Indios" realized how serious this European immigration problem was when Christobal's second trip to the new world included 17 ships, and 1,200 colonists with enough animals and supplies to build settlements. Following closely behind Columbus, in hopes of sharing in this new found free land, were the Dutch, English, French, and Swedish. Indios were then introduced to **"How it's gonna be!"**

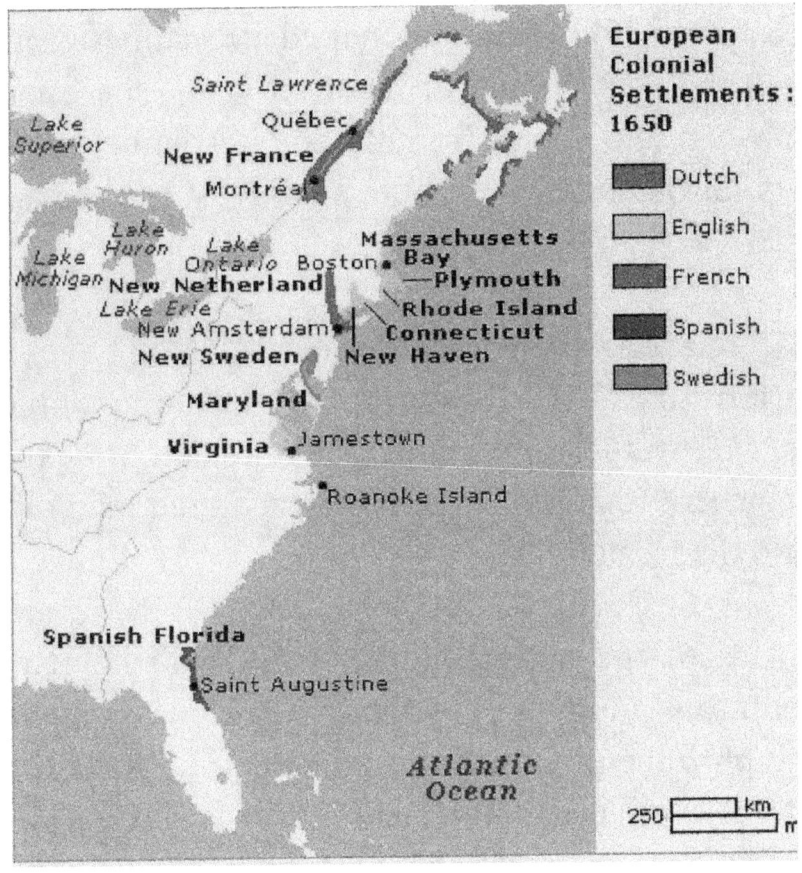

By 1650 newcomers had pretty well settled in.

These illegal invading European immigrants from far off countries colonized these new conquered lands with names like New France, New Netherlands, New Amsterdam, and New Sweden. I've often wondered what the native Indians called their lands before the white man took it away from them. The entire area eventually became known as New England.

The first Europeans to plant a flag on North American soil were the Spanish in 1565 when they settled in Saint Augustine in Florida. They called it Spanish Florida. Within the next couple of hundred years, the Spanish established settlements from the south Atlantic and Gulf coasts, through Texas and the southwest to the pacific coast.

New Englanders in the early 1880's in wanting to extend their territory to the Pacific Ocean picked a couple of guys, Meriwether Lewis and William Clark, to explore the northern region of their newly acquired land all the way to the western coast.

Along with the native Indian tribes who helped the adventurous duo, Lewis and Clark were able to accomplish their trek with the aide of a Shoshone Indian guide, a woman by the name of Sacagawea. Upon reaching the great Pacific Ocean, Lewis and Clark claimed all the lands they had crossed and surveyed as property of the United States.

Several other government sponsored expeditions soon followed Lewis and Clark's great discovery of the North West: Zebulon M. Pike and Stephen H. Long explored the central Great Plains – John C. Fremont covered the Rocky Mountains, Sierra Nevada and California – Robert Gray's maritime expeditions mapped the pacific coast including the mouth of the Columbia River strengthening the claim of the United States to the North West.

The geographic knowledge opened the way for not only trappers and mountain men like Jedediah Smith, but ordinary citizens to migrate to the far west to claim a piece of the government promised land for themselves. Between 1840 and 1860 more than a third of a million white folks moved from the Missouri Valley to the Pacific Coast. The discovery of gold in California sparked the gold rush of 1849 luring hundreds of thousands of more easterners to the gold fields.

The rush overwhelmed the Hispanic and Native Americans already living in California as whites killed Native Indians and took land claims from the Hispanics. Because of these conflicts over land rights, a war broke out between Mexico and the Anglo invaders. This Mexican American war was considered a straightforward land-grab. The ease and arrogance in which the United States won created a situation of distrust and sometimes violence at the southern border.

Whites must have been brought up believing they were indeed infallibly superior for they felt no remorse as they not only illegally took the land from theses natives of a darker hue, but enslaved, used, and abused them. This inbred feeling of superiority is still accepted and practiced on a regular basis by some white old schoolers.

As the flow of European immigrants continued to grow, the native Indians felt their freedom, dignity, and way of life rapidly disappearing. Unlike today's thinking, these poor Indians had no time to form a strong homeland security, or erect a barrier wall to keep out these unwanted illegals. So like good natives trying to protect what is theirs, they rebelled with force against the onslaught of white squatters who were trying to take over their land.

We all know the outcome of that rebellion as the defeated Indians were rounded up and forced to live on reservations scattered about the country. In today's attempt to eliminate segregation, and with a push for more equal rights, it's understandable why whites find it a bitter pill to swallow as they are forced to digest equality.

With the continuation of migration, the term race has rapidly became misunderstood and misused. It's often confused with the cultural differences derived from language, and ancestry.

For instants, immigrants of this country of European extraction are simply known and accepted as "White." Whereas people with a brown tinge to their pallor, originally from Spain or any other Spanish speaking country, are more likely to be called names like, Hispanic, Latino, Spic, or the catch all label of "Mexican." - Sometimes accompanied by the word "American."

Speaking of catch all, and adding to the confusion, is the modern day influx of immigrants coming from Central and South America. These poor individuals from all points south soon lose their true identity and are lumped in with the Mexicans. That is with the exception of the people from Spain who think they are of a purer blood line.

Well maybe they are! Because, unlike the Spanish elite with papers tracing their blue blood back to the main land, the rest of us Latinos are mongrels with wandering ways that have hooked up with just about anyone that would have us. I mean we've taken on all comers!

The largest part of the Mexican hookups has been mainly with the native Indios. This has created quite a mix of blood lines, pretty well thinning out the true Spanish in us. Most of us, who share a good resemblance to the native Indian, are isolated between the true Spaniard and the native Indian.

Here are a couple of examples of true Spanish nobility:

• Julio Inglesias, a Spaniard from Spain, while as a guest on the Johnny Carson Show, was referred to as a Mexican. To say Julio was a little indignant would be a gross understatement. He let it be known loud and clear, right there on stage, that he was a Spaniard and not a Mexican.

• My brother in-law, a true Spaniard from the bask area of Spain, was labeled a Mexican when he married my sister. I once asked him if he was offended in any way by this title. He said at first he was, but after many years of living with a Mexican family, he accepted the title of Mexican with pride. In fact he told me, whenever anyone asked him what his nationality was, he would proudly answer, "I'm a F—king Mexican."

Some people think Hispanics have a common genetic heritage, when in reality the only thing they share is a language. In contrast to this, and through out the world, other races like Asians and Blacks have multiple languages or dialects within their race. Even Whites, who share a common color, are separated by geographical areas and languages. Take European countries for instants whose people all share the same shade of beige, yet speak in different tongues.

Then there are the Natives of all the Americas, from the tip of Alaska to the bottom of South America, who share the European given title of "Indian." These Indians, separated by countries thousands of miles apart, and are divided by multiple languages and dialects, basically come from the same dye lot.

Even in this great country of ours, and much to the chagrin of Lou Dobbs and other think alike Anglos, there are many languages other than English spoken here – and that's not including the multiple dialects of each language. Like for instance the big difference between a Southern Drawl and Brooklynese.

This has made it difficult for those who persist in trying to make English the only legal language of the land. We must remember, and let us not forget, the South Western part of this country was originally a part of Mexico, with Spanish as its language. And another thing! What about Hawaii and Alaska? Should we ban their native language and insist they speak only English? **I don't think so!**

Speaking of Lou Dobbs, has he ever wondered why the European immigrants never bothered to learn the native Indian language when this country was invaded? I guess it was a lot easier to force the white mans language on them rather than learn the native languages.

With all that said and as a true American I believe for our good, and the good of this country, we should all speak a common language. With the popularity of the English language in this country, and through out the world, this should be the basic language taught to all cultures and ethnicities regardless of cultural and language ties to their Mama country.

I realize I just called myself a "True American." But how can that be, I have Mexican roots!

That's a good topic for the next chapter which happens to deal in what, why, and who is an...

"American"

Part Three

America!

Its origin, its inhabitants,

And who and what is an American?

According to the Encyclopedia International, America is the name used for the new world – basically consisting of the two continents, North and South America – also in the variously used regional names such as Central and Middle America. The encyclopedia also says it is incorrect to use the name America when used solely in reference to the United States. Other nations, specifically such as the ones north and south of us, feel they are a part of the Americas too!

Originally, America got its name in error by a French Cartographer Martin Waldseemuller, who made maps carving them out of wood. In 1507, in the process of making a map, Martin chiseled the name "America," on a land mass in the West Atlantic believing he was naming it after its discoverer "Amerigo Vespucci."

Amerigo was the ships captain who honestly believed he had discovered this new land mass which he originally thought was an island. It just so happened that the Island happened to be a large continent previously discovered by Columbus and is now known as South America. Martin Waldseemuller mistakenly carved the "A" of America right in the middle of Argentina.

This one and only rare map, made in error that gave America its name was purchased for $10 million and is on display at the Library of Congress. Years later (in 1513) Waldseemuller involved in carving out an atlas, tried to undo his error by renaming the same region "Terra Incognita." (Unknown land) Again, on a map published three years later, he called it "Terra Nova." (New world) It was all too late and in vain, the new land remained incorrectly named **"America."**

The Americas, North, Central and South America are divided into many nations with their own identity: Argentineans, Brazilians, Costa Ricans, etc. Our northern neighbors are called Canadians, and our southern neighbors are called Mexicans, The name United Statesians didn't go over too well and since there was no convenient adjective for the citizens of United States, the term American was and is customarily accepted by all. But, that's only when it pertains to Whites. All others are identified with their ethnicity included.

WHO AND WHAT IS AN AMERICAN

Back to Webster: *An American is a white guy that looks like Brad Pit and can play a German part in a war movie. An American gal usually fits the mold of the latest white teeny-bopper idol. Just kidding! (Or am I?) Webster really got it right this time, He says an American is a native or naturalized citizen of America.*

The United States, and its makeup of people, is almost as diverse as the rest of world. We've got'um coming from all over the globe in various shapes and colors. Before the big boats came from Europe and all points east, this was all Injun territory. With the arrival of the Gringos, the Spanish, and the French, this country was pretty well cut-up into three different sections - The Gringos in the east, the French in the middle, and the Spanish in the south and southwest.

The general image of an American in this country, though calling itself a melting pot, is usually of a fair complexioned individual primarily of European extraction. Coincidently the person creating this image of what an American should look like is usually done by fair complexioned individuals primarily of European extraction.

31

Speaking of American families how did this family sneak in? They look too ethnic to be an American family.

The Obamas – Barack, Michele - daughters Sasha & Malia

This picture of Barack Obama and his family appeared on the cover of People magazine published in August, 08' - Three months before the presidential election.

Mr. Obama, a black man of mixed parents, has set his goal on the white house – and by running for president has opened up quite a Pandora's Box! Like for Starters, what do we call this guy if he wins? Mr. Black American President?

Every president up to now has been a white guy. (We think) White guys and their families in the oval office are customarily and simply called Americans. And rightly so! But I hear in this country, if a guy has one small drop of black blood in him, he definitely is a Blackman or an African American.

As Mr. Obama campaigns for the office of the presidency, he is consistently referred to by news pundits as Black or African American. Yet, his republican counterpart, John McCain is never referred to as White or European American. In fact, in this country, McCain is just a regular American guy. You know…where his ethnicity is never mentioned and is none of anyone's business.

Ummm…Does this mean if Obama is elected to the presidency, he will no longer be constantly referred to as Black or African American? And does this also mean that as president he will finally be accepted as just a regular "All American Guy" with no reference to his ethnicity? **I don't think so!**

Speaking of all American, who really qualifies for this coveted title?   Here's an example of an individual and his family who do not qualify as "All Americans." Remember Mick Romney, one of the many that ran for the office of the presidency?   While ol' Mick was campaigning for the ultimate position in the country, he and his fair haired brood were referred to as the "All American Family."

That is until Keith Oberman on MSNBC, and his sneaky staff on "Countdown" discovered Romney's blood line had a little Mexican in it. Now with that bit of information shared with uptight America, Mr. Oberman declared publicly that Mick Romney's Mexican heritage disqualifies him and his family from the prestigious title of "All American." Whoa!!! What was Mick thinking?

Okay, enough about Barack and Mick and their search for the ever elusive American Dream - It's getting too confusing. Besides, there's more about Obama written in the political section of this book. Let's get back to the subject of newspaper ads and the image we've become familiar with as to what an American looks like.

Up to now, the American image has been well established as that of a fair haired and fare skinned society – an image that's been with us since Norman Rockwell was old enough to pick up a paint brush.

I once met Mr. Rockwell briefly in the 60's at the NBC studios in Burbank, California. He was being honored with a TV special for his great contribution to the world of Art. I was elated to meet the gentleman - a man I truly liked and admired. I have quite a collection of his works – composed mostly of books, and calendars. Sorry to say, no original paintings.

As an East LA Mexican, raised in the forties and fifties, I could never imagine myself as a typical American. This, I believe, came about because we had no Pancho Rockwell painting images of Mexicans and Indians as Americans. And because of the portrayal of only Easterners fitting the bill as Americans, Blacks, and Natives of the South West will always be considered different or foreign.

In looking at some typical illustrations that Norman painted for magazine covers such as "Colliers and Post," I was disappointed to note the lack of minorities in his paintings in which he portrayed the typical American family. This I believe is why, in thumbing though Norman's paintings, I never saw a picture of a Mexican, Black, or Asian portrayed as American. - Sorry, I used the word typical again!

However, I did find an interesting painting by Norman Rockwell with a little black girl in it!

This little black girl being escorted to school by federal officers was painted by Norman Rockwell for Look magazine in 1964. This was during the sixties when the south was going through its struggle with the newly enacted law of integration.

The West Coast, especially the southwest, has always been influenced by Easterners and how they perceive what America is all about. Take for instance Christmas and how we've been led to believe that Christmas is not Christmas unless it looks like New England. I remember as a kid having to paint snow in our windows to make it look more Christmassy. Why are we so strongly influenced in what easterners believe Christmas and anything else should look like? However, I did experience one white Christmas in 1955 when I was stationed in Wiesbaden Germany – **And man, it was beautiful!**

Since I've begun this topic on the types of people portrayed as Americans I've become more aware of the bigger range of color and ethnicities in the use of male and female models in advertisements.

We've come a long way from the fifties…

Where ads were only designed for white folks. In today's ads, you can now see a good mix of ethnicities. One recent "J.C. Penney" ad in particular caught my eye. It was of a young man of mixed parents, and a young lady of Hispanic origin. It's nice to see a collage of people and colors in ads that mirror our society more realistically. These multi-ethnic ads also include teens and children. Hopefully with these ads, and others like it, the face of this nation will no longer have one dominating look. Could you imagine a time when a persons color and ethnicity will be of no significance – To anyone!

The only ads I remember as a kid, were of white folks doing white things. This left the rest of us with just a hope that possibly someday we (Minorities) might just have a shot at being an average American eligible for the "American Dream."

White America decides who is an American

• When a young Boris Becker of Germany first came on the scene during the French tennis open, one sports announcer excitedly exclaimed, "Why he looks American!" I'm sure the comment by the announcer was influenced by the fact that Boris was tall, blond, and blue eyed. Using those features as a guideline to describe an American, the same thing could've been said about David Beckham, the international English soccer star. However...I'm not so sure the same thing would've been said of the dark skinned international soccer star "Pele."

• After the Viet Nam war, Mike Wallace did a segment for "Sixty Minutes" of orphans of mixed blood left behind by American GI's. As Mike walked about the streets singling out certain street urchins, he picked out only those kids with obvious European color and features. Mr. Wallace declared these kids as looking American. There were other orphans of obviously mixed ethnicities which Mr. Wallace neglected to mention.

These two stories of what is "American looking" sum up what we have been led to believe - and why we are comfortable with it.

Another factor in the debate of "whom and what" is an American, is how American or foreign sounding is ones name.

What's in a name?

What is an American sounding name you ask? Here are a few examples of famous Hispanic notables in the entertainment business who have managed to fool the system by changing or altering their names to sound more American:

- Rachel Welch – "Rachael Tejeda"
- Martin Sheen – "Ramon Estevez"
- Rita Hayworth – "Margarita Cansino"
- Henry Darrow – "Enrique Dominguez"
- Vickie Carr- "Victoria Cardenas
- Charlie Sheen – Carlos Estevez
- Gilbert Roland - ? (Mexican name)

Gilbert Roland, as a young Mexican who loved America and its movies, decided at a young age that he wanted to be in the movies. Figuring he would have more of a chance if he dropped his strong Mexican name and took on a new one, he decided to use the last names of his two favorite leading stars of the day – John Gilbert and Ruth Roland.

Then there are the biggies like John Wayne, Kirk Douglas, Burt Lancaster, and Cary Grant, who changed their names for obvious reasons. John Wayne's real name is Marrion Morrison and Cary Grant's given name is Archibald Leech. Could you imagine those names up on the marquee? And Kirk Douglas's real name sounds so foreign; he never would've made it through the studio gates.

With today's rebellious mood, some minorities prefer not to change their name and are satisfied with the name their mama and papa gave them. Two good examples of rebels are Christina Aguilera and the Editorial Columnist for the Daily News, Muriel Garza.

Christina, a singer and entertainer, is a fair looking lady born in the USA. She is very American looking - bleached blond and all! She is so American that as a kid she was a "Mouseketeer" in the popular all American television show "The Mickey Mouse Club." You can't get more American than that!

Rosie O'Donnell, TV show hostess, commented on Christina Aguilera's foreign sounding name and asked her if she was going to change it to a more American sounding name. A surprised Christina, asked Rosie why she would ever ask such a question - and NO, she had no desire to ever change her name.

Realizing her mistake, Rosie embarrassedly changed the subject and did not bring it up again. Rosie, a typical Irish American born in the USA, automatically assumes her last name of "O'Donnell" as an American name. She also insinuates that Christina's last name of Aguilera, also born in the USA, is a foreign name. Rosie's show was taped in the San Fernando Valley, (Hispanic Name) in the city of Los Angeles, (Hispanic name) and in the state of California. (Also a Hispanic name) Who has the foreign sounding name here?

Rosie, a good entertainer and a great TV host, forgets that all names in this country are foreign sounding. But Rosie, like so many other whites of European extraction, is under the illusion that she and her likes have exclusive rights to the title of American.

Next is Muriel Garza a columnist for the Los Angeles Daily News. Muriel, a light haired blue eyed lady, never consciously denied her Latina roots, but when she did reveal in her column that she was a Mexican American, she was surprised at the amount of mail she received in response - Most of it hate mail. She assumed, with a name like Garza, her readers would take it for granted that she was Hispanic. I personally wrote her a letter of the importance of an American sounding name. I reminded her, in order to get along in the business; all she had to do was alter her name to "Garr."

And another thing, how come Jennifer Lopez and Alex Rodriguez aren't referred to publicly by their given names? Since Lopez and Rodriguez have come on the scene with such a high profile, society has seen fit to tag them with names that are something less ethnic – Like "J-Lo" and "A-Rod."

Is it because the names Lopez and Rodriguez were too Mexican sounding? Or is it simply that this country is not ready to accept the popular Hispanic names of Lopez and Rodriguez as typically important American names.

Could you imagine Jennifer Anniston being tagged with the nick-name of "J-Ann." - Or Mark McGuire as M-Mc? Let's just push it a little further and include Babe Ruth as "B-Ru" – I don't think so! Is it just me, or are there others out there with my simple kind of thinking?

Remember back in the old days when Fernando Valenzuela, Ace-pitcher for the Dodgers, came on the scene? Well I do! I recall two sports announcers having a problem with Fernando's last name. After a short discussion, and as if he was some kind of a pet, they took it upon themselves to come up with a nick name for him. Fernando was playing baseball in a stadium built in the city of Los Angeles on a site originally called "Chavez" Ravine."

And how about those black people who were brought here in chains? How did they get their names? I hear some of them were given the names of their owners, while others took the names of presidents; Like Lincoln, Jefferson, and Washington. I know this for a fact because my sister-in-law told me so.

This story involving my sister-in-law dates back to the seventies when this country, with prodding from the government, had to get on the integration kick. With workforces out of racial balance and purely out of embarrassment, The Government instructed businesses to hire enough minorities to fill a designated quota.

My sister-in-law, (A white girl) was given a list of bank employees and asked to record the number of minorities in the company. She was also asked to separate them by ethnicities. It was easy recognizing Hispanic and Asian names, but when it came to African American names - that was another thing!

Scratching her head in confusion, she asked her boss, "How could she tell who was African American simply by looking at the list of employees?" She was told to list those with presidential names such as Lincoln, Washington, and Jefferson as African American. She agreed and did what she was told.

However, when she married my Mexican brother-in-law, she was surprised to find out that because of her new last name, she was now a Hispanic employee! With the changing of her name to a Mexican name, she lost her white identity, along with the perks that go with it.

Certain names, like most English and Irish names, without question are considered typically American. Also acceptable are Scandinavian and Germanic names - As long as they are pronounceable! Then we have Italian names, which in this country are somewhere in limbo. With the exception of a name like Sinatra which is a name as American as apple pie!

Then we have a confused Geraldine Ferraro - An Italian lady who was once a candidate for the Vice Presidency of the United States. She doesn't have a clue as to whom or what she is. In the presidential election of 2008 Miss Ferarro, stated publicly the only reason Barack Obama got to be a candidate for the office of the presidency was because he was "Black!"

Now why she called Barack Obama Black I'll never know. Didn't she know he's half white? And to give her comment more credibility Geraldine proclaimed she was "White." Sounds to me like just another Italian chick passing her self off as White.

44

To clarify Geraldine's confusion, let's go back and see what Webster has to say about Italians. Whoa!!! Surprise, surprise…according to Webster; a female of Italian heritage is a Latina! "Wow, a Latina - better not tell her that!" Just think what her friends would say if they found out she was a "Minority." Heck, if I would've known she was a Chicana when she ran for Vice President, I would've voted for her!

Italians, (Latinos) seem to slip unnoticed right through the "Whites only" gates, no matter how ethnic looking they are, or how Italian sounding their name is. But unlike Italian names, Mexican names are considered by some as a negative thing. Mexicans, (Latinos) in this country with strong ethnic names like Lopez or Rodriguez, will always have a problem crossing any gate.

The negativities of some ethnic names are important – especially when it deals with a person's happiness and composure on a daily basis. Here are a couple of examples:

A White female friend of mine married a guy named Delgado. They lived happily in a white neighborhood with their two kids. The only problem was the abusive teasing that their kids received from schoolmates for having a Mexican name. The school kids made the Delgado kids cry by chanting their name as "Del-Taco."

Another example of a negative name concerns the White wife of a co-worker of mine who married a guy named Hernandez. She once told me she was not proud, and somewhat embarrassed, by the name Hernandez. As a white blond girl she felt very conscientious about saying her last name. She wished her last name wasn't so typically Mexican sounding. She wished it was more like my name, Obregon.

Obregon is a name right out of Mexico. There was a presidential hero by the name of Obregon who had a city named after him. For some reason the name Obregon has never been questioned as a negative thing. Maybe I should be thankful for having an uncommon name. Minorities, besides daily jousts with racism, must also contend with names which to some, are considered un-American.

Another race of people, who at one time were minorities, is the Irish. They've come a long way from their meager beginnings. They are now certified white Americans. Just ask them, they'll tell you. One Irish guy, Pat Buchanan a political analyst, and author, while on one of his book promoting tours, in speaking about People of color, referred to them by their ethnicity: Chinese American, African American, etc. One individual in the audience snidely asked, "By your standard of classifying people by their ethnicity, would you consider yourself a **"European American?"**

After a nervous chuckle of disbelief, Pat, an Irish Catholic American, quickly responded with, "I prefer to be called White." Mr. Buchanan, who was one of President Nixon's advisors and a candidate for the Presidency himself, speaks for most descendants of Europe as to his preference of being called a White American.

Speaking of Irish Catholics, Chris Matthews, host of "Hard Ball" on MSNBC, once called himself a minority? Oh, yeah!!! Honest! The subject was on the various minority groups in this country. He was reminiscing about the old days when Irish immigrant families lived in the slums and were considered second class citizens. (Minorities)

After a moment in thought, he softly mentioned that this was the first time he had ever considered himself a minority. Hey maybe there's hope for the rest of us after all. Could you imagine sometime in the future where Blacks, Hispanics, and Asians have to take a trip down memory lane to recall their days as minorities?

My family has a history in the Southwest dating back to 1818 - when it was Spain! My mother, born in Tempe, Arizona in 1892 and a mother of ten always tried to instill in us kids that we were Americans and not Mexicans. She strongly felt it would be advantages to us if we truly believed we were Americans.

She thought by convincing us we were Americans, we would feel entitled to the same rights and privileges as white folks. But despite my mother's constant preaching, and my seventh grade teacher, white America rejects us beaners as Americans as they continue to label us as Mexican or Mexican American.

In the early fifties, while filling out a high school entry form, I was surprised to see Mexican, along with White, Black, and Asian as an option for race. I questioned the administrator as to why the word Mexican was officially referred to as a race. "When did Mexican become a Race?" I asked. Without looking up, and with a voice of authority replied, "It's for identification purposes only."

At that moment in time I realized as a native Californian, of Hispanic heritage, my race was now officially Mexican. And as a Mexican, I would never be eligible to be an American. However, under certain circumstances, I may be referred to as a "Mexican American."

Because of this strong and constant reminder that I am not an American, I have never really thought of myself as one. During the 2000 census, where the questioner gave so many options as to what I was, I wrote a letter voicing my objection to the many options published in the Los Angeles Times.

Milestone for mixed races (3-16-00) and the opening line "For the first time a person can check two or more ethnicities." My Mexican roots, which I am proud of, date back to when the southwest was still Mexico. Being of a culture that is over labeled now, I disagree with the census takers adding more options. My identity has always been a flavor of the month type of thing. As a youngster, my mother, and seventh grade teacher, tried in vain to convince me I was an American. My school chums, along with the School Board, corrected them by tagging me as Mexican. During my rebellious teenage years, I proudly claimed the title of Chicano. The Army dubbed me Caucasian. A major corporation listed me as "Other." In legalese, I'm referred to as Hispanic. Now, as a recent retiree, the census bureau adds to my confusion, and ask me to pick one or more identities from a multiple of names, including Spanish - Hispanic - Latino - Mexican, - Mexican American, - Chicano, etc. My education tells me my race is Caucasian, my nationality American, and my heritage, which is only relevant to myself, should not be a factor in this country of freedom and equality. Your article and the census itself, contradict our forefathers intent. This country has always been referred to as a melting pot for all races and ethnicities, for the sole purpose of blending into a unique and special existence

Albert Obregon

Whites, who have enjoyed the perks of whiteness since the inception of this country, find it unacceptable to see or acknowledge minorities as equal Americans. This is where the problem lies. It appears they (whoever "THEY" are) prefer tagging us with labels like Hispanic, and Latino instead of American.

Then there are those not so nice in their name calling who prefer unsavory names like Spic, Beaner, Wetback, or the simple title of "Mexican" – which to some is a derogatory thing. This leads us to our next big question; when did the word Mexican become a derogatory thing?

Why Mexican is a derogatory thing?

In the nineteen-nineties, during the murder trail of O.J. Simpson, Johnnie Cochran (Attorney for OJ) spouted that Mark Furman (a Los Angeles Police Officer) was a racist by referring to people of color as "Niggers" and "Mexicans." This was said in a public court during a high profile trail. I remember thinking at the time of the lack of attention given to Mr. Cochran's comment and how no eyebrows or questions were raised when he declared that calling a person a Mexican is akin to calling an African American a "Nigger!"

On a lighter side, on a favorite show of mine "The Office," entertainer Steve Carroll, who plays Michael on the show, asked Oscar Martinez one of his employees, if he would prefer to be called something less offensive than Mexican.

"Mexican isn't offensive," replied the employee.
"Well it has certain connotations."
"What kind of connotations Michael?"
Michael suddenly excused himself to do more important stuff.

Being of a curious mind, I've often questioned myself as to why this negative connotation exists? Why does the word Mexican give off such a bad vibe? So once again I called on my buddy Webster for some rhyme or reason to it all.

Webster has an array of definitions relating to the brown race.

Mex-i-can /'mek-si-kan **a:** A native or inhabitant of Mexico **b:** A person of Mexican descent. **c** *Southwest:* a person of mixed Spanish and Indian descent.

Hispanic: *Relating to people or culture of Spain, Portugal or Latin America* - This takes in a broad range which could fit just about anybody in the nation.

Spic: Spanish American – Mexican – usu: **taken to be offensive.** To this day, and for the life of me, I have yet to find the origin of the word Spic.

Latino, Latin - Latimus from *Labium,* the district of Italy in which Rome was built. Pertaining to Latins. Latin races, the Italians, French, Spanish, etc.

Then, to add to the confusion, many Mexicans have American sounding names. Take the name of "Richardson" for instance. You hear that name, and right away you think of a white guy from middle America (wherever that is). But one Mexican guy named Bill Richardson, a Hispanic from New Mexico, defines himself as a Latino, with a white name, who happens to look Indian. This Indian looking guy named Richardson competed for the nomination of the Democratic Party in the presidential race of 2008.

In discussing Richardson ethnicity, one of the guests on a panel on the Fox News Network said, "He doesn't look Hispanic." Its observations like this from so-called mainstream white America that keeps the stereotypical image of what a Hispanic should look like. A funny thing about images, when I was young and dumb, I was led to believe that an American was a tall white good looking blond person with a pretty smile. Now who could've convinced me of that…Huh?

Speaking of images, while painting and aging a Mexican restaurant for one of the sets on a TV soap opera, the Art Director insisted we make it dirtier with a lot more grime on the set. I questioned the Art Director, "Why so much grime? There are nice Mexican restaurants too!" His answer, without much thought was, "Because that's what the people in Ohio think a Mexican restaurant looks like."

Once again we have a stereotypical image of what middle class Americans wish to believe Mexicans are like. This negative portrayal of Hispanics, that continues to go unchecked, is a verification of what the white majority believes. But like most ethnicities, Hispanics come in all shapes and colors. Their looks vary from a very fair and pretty Ricky Martin, to the dark ugly guy who played opposite Humphrey Bogart in "Treasure of Sierra Madre." Remember him? He's the scarred faced rotten toothed "Bandito."

This bandito was mostly famous for his portrayal of a guy pretending to be the leader of the federales who said, **"Badges ...we don't need no estinking badges."** With these two examples of Ricky Martin and the Bandito, guess who mainstream America most identifies Hispanics with. Yup...you guessed it! The Bandito!

This brings to mind, years ago, a "Fritos" commercial portrayed a little cartoon character by the name of "The Frito Bandito." This was before political correctness when you could get away with cute tag names like "Little Black Sambo."

On Bill Moyer's Journal, a PBS Special that aired February 8, 08, Rev. Samuel Rodriguez, a guest on the show, explained his thoughts on the subject of "what is an American." He said he was once told to "Tell your people (Latinos) to embrace the American culture and become Americans."

Mr. Rodriguez eloquent response was, "What does it mean to be an American? Does that mean White American? Anglo-Saxon - European? To me an American is an individual who looks at the documents of our founding fathers - The Declaration of Independence, the Bill of Rights and the Constitution and says, "These are my values!

I not only adopt these values I adhere to these values - They're mine! It's not the color of your skin - your language - your accent - or your vernacular. It's whether or not these values become your values. That's American! I call it the American Covenant." Rev. Samuel Rodriguez is the President of the National Hispanic Christian Leadership Conference which claims eighteen thousand churches as members. Newsweek Magazine identified him as an up and coming leader.

Reverend Rodriguez pretty well nails it idealistically as to what an American should be. But, realistically we are reminded on a regular basis as to what an American is. Most whites would agree that these little brown people of Spanish origin are generally simple and feeble minded – only capable of stoop labor and menial tasks. President Nixon, while in office, confirmed what most whites believe by stating, "Those people (Mexicans) are physically built for stoop labor, mainly for picking crops."

This unbelievable comment, coming from the president, did not get the attention or negative press it deserved. With Nixon's personal observation of the physical structure and purpose of the Mexican people, is it any wonder why minorities are considered and treated like second class citizens.

A very good friend and co-worker of mine (Anglo) once asked me if I knew the name of the "Mexican boy" working in the tool room. This Mexican boy that my friend was referring to was a forty-two year old man with a prominent position. After answering my friend by telling him the name of the forty-two year old Mexican boy, and out of pure curiosity, I asked him if he knew the name of the "White boy" working in the Drapery Department.

Looking at me in disbelief my friend asked, "How could you call him a boy?" I in turn thought to myself, "Why did I call the forty two year old white man a boy?" The question as to the name of the Mexican boy working in the tool room, when asked by my Anglo friend, appeared normal and natural to me. It is rather common to hear Anglos refer to male minorities as "boy" - regardless of their age.

But when I asked the same question by calling a white person of the same age a boy, it appeared awkward and demeaning. Imagine how confused my friend would've been if I had used the ethnicity of the guy working in drapery by asking, "What is the name of the Scottish boy that works in drapery?" The title word "Boy" is still used by many Whites in reference to minorities in some geographical and social levels of society.

My friend, like most white folks, is an intelligent and well educated individual with a good soul who would never <u>intentionall</u>y demean anyone of any race or color

Once again we have a product socially and environmentally programmed to be a superior white.

Next chapter is simply on Racism in all aspects.

Part Four

RACISM

It's a funny thing this thing called racism - Are we genetically born with it? Did our mama's and papa's teach us to hate those unlike us in color or culture? Or has life taught us to use racism as part of our survival in this competitive world? Contrary to the popular phrase "I am not a racist," by some notables, we are all racist to some degree - Which degree we opt to practice racism is our own personal choice.

When the white man first set foot on this land, claiming all he surveyed, he assumed all rights of authority thus rendering the darker skinned natives to a lesser level. This self-proclaimed authority was based on the white factor that darker people, with a **different** look, are at odds in behavior, attitude, intelligence, or intrinsic worth. With that kind of thinking, **is it any wonder why there is so much...**

Racism against people of color

Through out history, and in his endeavor for power and position, man has proven how cruel and inhumane he can be over his fellow man. When the European immigrants first came to this country some of them brought their own servants with them.

This custom of legal and regulated indentured servitude, practiced in the old country, was brought over here by immigrants accustomed to having people of a lesser value do their bidding. This came about when poor Europeans, wanting to escape the harsh conditions of Europe, voluntarily sold four to seven years of their lives for free passage to America. But like most good things - they have to end.

As the new American colonies grew and prospered, there was a bigger demand for more indentured servants. But for some reason in the 17th century, there was a sharp decline of servant migration. This shortage of available help created a labor crisis. So white folks, being white folks, did what white folks usually do when there's work to be done – they became resourceful and got somebody else to do it.

Consequently to meet this labor shortage in the 1680's, landowners turned to using slaves imported from Africa. **"Imported"** - That might be too nice a word to use – **"They were brought here against their will in chains!"**

The transatlantic slave trade produced one of the largest forced migrations in history. From the early 16th century to the mid-19th century, more than 10 million Africans were taken from their homes and crammed into packed ships where they were shipped to the Americas. Upon arrival to the new strange land, and still in chains, Africans were put on the auction block to be sold.

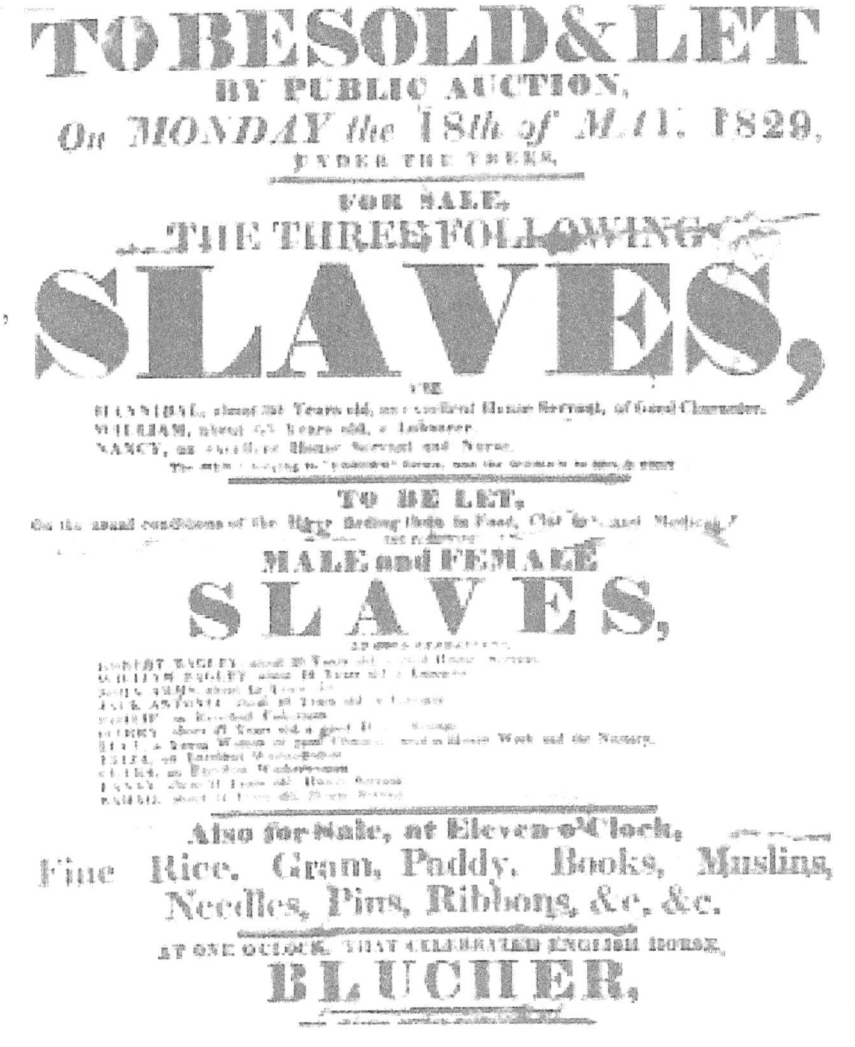

Most slaves transported to America came from the west-central coast of Africa. In North America the first African slaves, brought over on Dutch ships, landed in Jamestown, Virginia in 1619. They were either sold or rented, depending on the land owner's situation or needs.

Often these slave auctions separated family members from one another; creating a situation where some would never see each other again. Slavery was a very popular thing in its day – In fact; eight of our first twelve Presidents owned slaves.

When the civil war was over and slavery was abolished, there was a strong attempt by the whites to re-slave the Negro. A system was created to corral the newly freed Negros and keep them under the white man's rule. This system was called "Black Code." Negros, labeled shiftless and lawless, were arrested under newly created laws specifically designed to incarcerate them.

Most blacks, omitted from the legal process and unable to show proof of employment or residence, were usually charged and arrested for vagrancy. These black prisoners were first placed into chain gangs, *(Back in your chains guys!)* then sold or traded to labor camps where they were forced to work without compensation. The white man once again had his legal slavery - this time it was much more profitable.

Information for the last two paragraphs was gathered from an interview on PBS's Bill Moyers Journal (6-20-08) featuring a White author by the name of Douglas Blackmon.

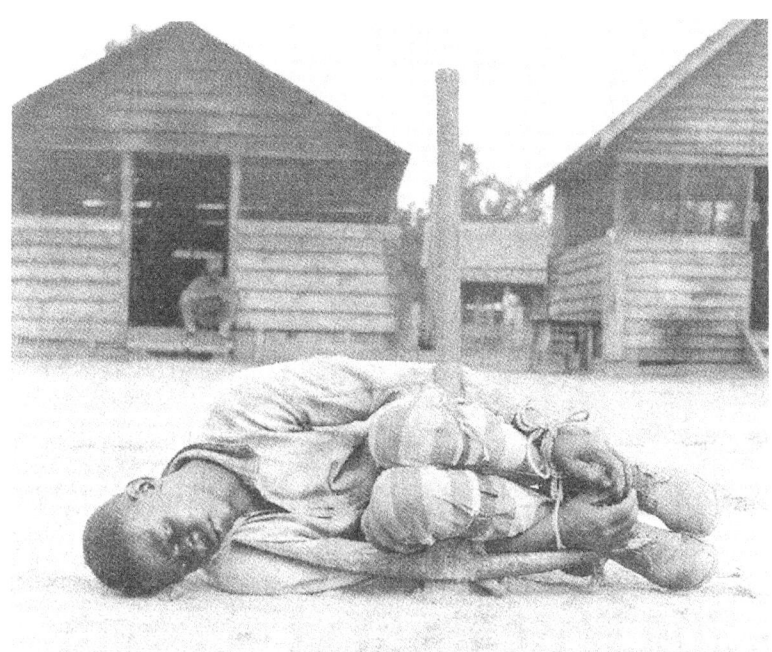

Post-Civil War Slavery

Long after the Civil War's final shots were fired, hundreds of thousands of African-Americans were held captive and forced to work hard labor without compensation. Douglas Blackmon, the author of a new book, explains how "neoslavery" continued into the 1940s, and narrates a slide show of photographs from the era, at xtra.Newsweek.com

This photo of a black man on a chain gang, tied to a pick and put on display, pretty well displays how far we've sunk in our inhumanity towards man."

Most White southern fortunes were made under this system of industrial slavery. These big land barons eventually became the big financial capitalists of today. I'm sure we've all heard the expression, "That family comes from old southern money." You'll never hear that said about any blacks – the ones that built and worked the businesses.

Whites, historically, have taken care of whites. As the newly freed slaves were floundering for existence, their previous owners were compensated by the government for their loss of revenue. When Moyers asked Douglas Blackmon, why most Americans were unaware of this type of negative History, his response was, "Because of the cruel and inhumane way Negros were treated, white historians chose to limit or ignore this negative part of History."

 Negros, because of "Black Code," have always been suspicious and untrusting of the white man and his law. Also included in the "Not trusting the white man club" are the Native Americans, who were subjected to a bunch of lies and a slew of broken treaties.

Unlike the days of slavery when racism was practiced legally, openly, and regularly, today's society is apt to be less blatant and more subtle in its continued practice of racism. Batteries of corporate attorneys have gotten rich explaining and defending theses subtleties.

Few of our American history books have revealed how blacks in the early years were seriously mistreated. But from the time slavery was abolished in the 1860s' to the 1930's Whites, whether inherently or defiantly, were unable to adjust to cohabitating with the newly freed Negros. They could not see blacks ever being equal with whites.

This is where the KU-KLUX-KLAN came in. A white supremacist group that hid under sheets, and with torches in hand, proceeded to terrorize the newly freed Negro. Thousands of these freed slaves were violently expelled from their homes and land. The following factual information was taken from a 2008 PBS special entitled "Banished."

• 1864 - Washington County, Indiana - Blacks were told to "Leave town or die!"

• 1901- Pierce City, Missouri - A black teen was accused of raping and killing a white girl. He was lynched in the public square, and two of his family members were burned for good measure. Still unsatisfied, the white folks of Pierce City took up arms and standing on the street that bordered the black neighborhood, fired their guns into Black homes forcing blacks to abandon their homes and property. To this day, Pierce City has been able to maintain their all white citizenry.

One hundred years later in 2001, descendants of these black families returned to Pierce city to reclaim their property. Their pleas of reclamation were received sympathetically from all concerned authorities - but without satisfaction. This was the same story of many rejected descendants of southern Blacks.

• 1905 - In Harrisburg, Arkansas - Black citizens were twice kicked out of their homes with two waves of white terror. *Harrisburg, like Pierce City, has maintained an all white city.*

• 1909 - Forsyth, Georgia - Whites took to bombing black homes forcing more than a thousand blacks to abandon their homes and flee.

Since the early nineteen hundreds, Blacks have been subjected to various degrees of racial abuse. It was during the 50's and 60's where racial tensions between Blacks and Whites finally came to a head. Blacks, fed up with the years of "Whites" deciding their fate, took integration into their own hands. They used peaceful organized boycotts and sit-ins to express their disgust and disapprovals of "whites only" restaurants and diners. The news of Southern whites retaliating against the Black sit-ins with dogs, fire hoses and Billy clubs, forced the government to act.

Little Rock, Arkansas - 1957

In 1957, in Little Rock Arkansas, Governor Orval Faubus, in defiance of court rulings ordering racial integration, sent in the National Guard to prevent black students from entering white city schools. President Dwight Eisenhower responded by sending in federal troops to take over and provide safe passage for Black kids entering their local schools. Can you believe it - A racist Governor using the National Guard to keep Blacks from attending an all white school?

In 1962, in Mississippi, Governor Ross R. Barnett ignored a court order by the U.S. Supreme Court ordering the University of Mississippi to admit a black student James Meredith into their institution - The first black student to ever enroll in the University.

Despite President Kennedy's plea for the people of Mississippi to obey the law, a riot broke out lasting fifteen hours and causing two deaths. Kennedy sent in federal troops to restore order and ensure that Meredith was admitted to the school. The troops and federal marshals stayed on campus to ensure his safety.

Before he was assassinated, Kennedy used his time in office trying to fix the civil rights problem. He particularly wanted to end discrimination in federally financed projects and in companies doing business with the government. The Black rebellion against inhumane treatment, brought on by discrimination, became pretty well spread.

Five years later (S' 1967) and because of the continued urban racial issues, several riots broke out in major U.S. cities. The first big one happened in Newark on July 12 when rumors spread that police had killed a Negro cab driver. Five days later, with the help of state troopers, the rioting was brought under control. When the smoke cleared, there were 26 people dead, with an estimated property damage of $30 million.

More than 300 fires were set leveling entire blocks in the main district area. It was the worst outbreak of racial violence since the 1965 Watts riots in Los Angeles. Ten days after Newark, on July 27, a bigger riot broke out in Detroit killing over 40 people. (Blacks and whites) This time Federal troops were used to quell the civil uprising. There were almost fifteen hundred fires set leaving 5,000 homeless.

The seriousness of the Detroit race riot, forced President Lynden Johnson to halt the melee by sending in the Army to quell the uproar. Before the riot was brought to a halt, more than 400 persons were arrested with damages estimated at $250-500 million. In that same year (1967) there was a total 126 other riots in cities scattered thru-out the country, 75 of those riots were major.

Because of this rash of riots President Lyndon Baines Johnson, in order to keep the pot from boiling over, established a commission to find out what was sparking these riots.

The commission's goal was to find out three things:
- **What happened**
- **Why did it happen**
- **And what can be done to prevent this from happening again.**

The Commission titled "National Advisory on Civil Disorder," headed by Otto Kerner, included the Mayor of New York, John Lindsey and Senator Fred Harris. This study published in 1968 was later referred to as the "Kerner Commission."

The commission's findings basically found that,

"WHITES WERE RESPONSIBLE" FOR THE RIOTS"

These findings, of the commission, were both surprising and disappointing to President Johnson. He was sure there was a conspiracy behind the riots, and that the Black Panthers were involved in one way or another.

Adding to the President's chagrin were the findings concluding that the riots were stemmed from racism, poverty, and the continued injustice suffered by Blacks. Senator Harris, of the original Kerner Commission, in 2008 as a guest on PBS's Bill Moyer's Journal, spoke out at length of what the commission had discovered. This was a good reminder to us all of how much further we had to go.

The following are Newspaper Headlines influenced by the results of Kerner Commission report.

- "Racism deeply embedded in American society."

- "What white Americans have never fully understood – but what the Negro can never forget - is that the white society is deeply implicated in the ghetto."

- "White institutions created it, White institutions maintain it, and White institutions condign it."

- "Our nation is moving towards two societies – one white, one black – separate and unequal."

This all happened during the sixties when this "Separate and unequal" condition was considered to be a temporary situation - but here we are in the new millennium, and we still can't get it right! Could it be that certain individuals just don't want to get it right – especially those in position who historically have enjoyed their power and have no intention of ever correcting this obvious wrong?

Anyway, in 1967 during the time of the riots, another incident occurred involving a controversial character by the name of Martin Luther King Jr.

Because of Mr. King's history of leading civil rights movements, and his strong belief in speaking truth to power, he was singled out as an instigator for the riots and arrested on a 1963 contempt of court charge in Birmingham, Alabama.

Mr. King, because of his strong believe in racial equability, was often abused, beaten, and jailed for his stance against the treatment of blacks. While incarcerated, Martin Luther King Jr. wrote his famous Birmingham jail letter. He was assassinated in 1968.

White Americans were not really willing to accept a united and equal society; they still preferred the way of the sixties with its "separate and unequal" theme. But with pressure from blacks wanting equality, and a government forced to comply, there was a movement to integrate our schools. One big question they had to deal with was, **"How do you appease whites without denying blacks their rights."**

Bussing was one of the most common methods of desegregating school districts. Both Whites and Blacks, were bussed from school to school, to integrate schools that otherwise would be either all white or all black.

There is so much more I could write on the subject of blacks and their plight for equality, but I must get on with this chapter and the struggles of other minorities and their Racist problems. Because of my limited research and education, some minorities might not get the attention and sympathy they truly deserve.

Come to think of it, what is a racist?

Is a racist a person who simply hates those of another color or culture? Like the hooded vigilantes of old who terrorized the southern blacks? Most would agree, including southern whites, that the Ku-Klux-Klan was a racist organization. Whites also agree and believe that racism is a thing of the past and really doesn't affect us anymore - therefore we don't need federal programs like affirmative action which only complicate matters.

Whites in general have a problem recognizing racism while minorities, who deal with it on a regular basis, have a built-in-radar for detecting xenophobia. As an observant minority in my seventies, I feel well qualified in spotting racism in any form: from the obvious hooded Klan to the subtle actions, moods, and code words used by whites. It usually can be detected daily in most contacts, whether they are socially or business related.

To know the true fear and anxiety of intimidation when confronted by a ruling and unfavorable majority is something most whites will never truly understand - To have to live and become the compliant subservient with the broad smile and glad hand for the purpose of survival.

However, there have been some rare cases and circumstances where whites have had to taste the bitterness of a minority status. Like for instance, the movie "The Grand Canyon" where Kevin Klein finds himself stranded at night in the wrong side of town surrounded by a gang of black toughs. I'll never forget Kevin's portrayal of a man who, under such intimidating circumstances, accepts his new less than equal status. In watching Kevin's willingness to go along passively with his new role as a minority, the realization came to me; "This is what minorities deal with in life on a regular basis."

Racism and the American Indian

For thousands of years Native Americans have enjoyed this land of plenty as they roamed about as free men. This all came to a crashing halt when the first white immigrant set foot on American soil and decided to stay a while. Because of their darker skin, the Native Americans were considered less human by the whites, so they enslaved the Indians and used them to build their settlements.

Most American history books (written by white men) dealing with the early pioneers and how the West was won, kinda lean toward the white man's side. The stories we've heard and the movies we've seen, traditionally, while portraying the Indians as cowardly brutal savages, make the white man look brave and heroic. And why is it if Indians win, it's a massacre, but when the white guy wins, the words victory and bravery, come up a lot in the report.

You'd think the white man would'a been content in taking enough land on the eastern coast, but no, they weren't satisfied with just having a part of something – they wanted it all! - Regardless of the consequences to whomever got in the way. So in their passion for more land, and the advice of Horace Greeley's "Go west young man," white guys saddled their horses and rode west to do some shopping.

Some of the things they desired were not on the market, but they took them anyway. Their greedy and bold aggression created some ill will with the local natives leading to some major disputes.

In settling a lot of these disputes, the white man came up with treaties designed to pacify the Indian - treaties which the Indians placed their complete trust in. These treaties were the basis for all new incoming Europeans to secure peace with the natives while trying to steal their land. History guys can't agree on how many treaties there were, but it was estimated to be well into the thousands.

The first exploring conquistadores to the new world, believing the natives were heathen or subhuman, needed no treaties as they ruthlessly took the land they wanted. But by the 1540s a Spanish cleric, Francisco de Vitoria, convinced the Spanish crown and its explorers, that the natives were indeed human.

So now instead of taking the Indians land by conquest, they had to be nice and treat these guys with respect. This is where treaties were implemented to con the natives into trusting the white man. But with so much land and resources, the white man couldn't control himself. As history has revealed, while all the treaties were violated in some form or another, most of them were broken.

The invading white man never really had any intention of cohabitating with the darker skinned savages – Not with so much land and riches to be had? Are you kidding? Then came the famous cry…

"There's Gold in them thar' hills."

With the discovery of gold in the west, came a rush of illegal whites seeking their fortune. These claim-jumping European immigrants came west with a prospecting shovel in one hand and a gun in the other - AND heaven help the Indian or Mexican that got in their way. In fact the battle of the Little Big Horn, where Custer met his maker, began with the discovery of gold in the Black Hills of Wyoming.

This same thing happened in Georgia when gold was discovered. Blacks were harassed by the usual means of verbal threats, and physical attacks by whites, forcing Blacks to leave their homes and property. This is another good example of how whites through out our history have acquired most, if not all, of the wealth by hook or crook.

Then again in the Southwest where the Indians and Mexicans lived, the invading whites took property and anything else they wanted from the darker skinned natives. I guess this answers the question as to how come most of the properties of the Southwest have Spanish and Indian names – but are owned by Whites.

As been stated, History books and most movies depicting how the west was won, have systematically told the story from a white mans point of view. This usually depicts the Indians or American Natives as savages without conscience. Simply put: **"Wild Indians"**

Next comes the ...eh. Mexicans **(I theenk)**

Now these poor guys have no idea who and what they are – and more importantly, where they belong!

As a kid born in East Los Angeles, California I never really knew who or what I was. My mama repeatedly told me that I was an American. Yet all my school mates and friends more or less convinced me I was a Mexican. This has always been a confusing issue to me. I think my mother was wrong! How could I be an American, if I didn't have blond hair or blue eyes like a gringo?

Even my seventh grade teacher got into the act by pulling a spot quiz on us students. She asked each of us to write down our place of birth, and our nationality. The teacher was both surprised and upset when she told us how wrong we all were. Handing back our papers she said, "There is only one of you in this class who knows what nationality he really is." That person happened to be a black kid from back east someplace. On the other hand, like most of the students in class, I wrote down I was a Mexican born in Los Angeles.

Let's go back to the beginning and see how this all became so confusing and just how did these "Beaners" get here anyway? Believe it or not, they've always been here – I mean, since the sixteenth century when Spain colonized large portions of the United States.

According to early historical maps, Spain owned a big chunk of the new world which included: All of the Southwestern United States – Central America – and portions of South America. In fact in 1588, at the height of its power, Spain was one of the richest and most powerful countries of the world.

That is until the eighteen hundreds when the greedy white gringos wanted a bigger chunk of the Americas. In 1845 the United States annexed the Republic of Texas which had recently won its independence from Mexico. A dispute over the location of the Texas border created a tense situation between the United States leading to the Mexican War of 1846. This conflict was viewed by many as an unnecessary war perpetrated by the land-hungry whites.

In 1848, the Treaty of Guadalupe Hidalgo was signed ceding the territory of what is now the American Southwest. Mexico's great Territorial losses cut their dreams short as they realized the United States would now become the predominate power in North America.

Many native Southwest Mexicans deeply resented their loss to the invading Gringos. With their loss came the realization that they no longer would share in the decision making of their future. They would now have to step back as subservient guests. These new brown citizens of the United States, in doubt as to whom and what they were, found it difficult adapting to the white man's ways.

This dilemma of the social status of the native Mexicans even confused the white folks. They couldn't call them Mexicans cause it was no longer Mexico – And they couldn't call them Indians or Black people cause they weren't! So what should they do? They decided to do nothing and let the racist take over. And that's exactly what the racist did – they took over.

Mexicans were pretty well discriminated against in the southern western states - Especially in Texas where whites proudly hung up signs reading "No Dogs, Niggers or Mexicans allowed."

The Mexicans, who were treated as non-whites just like the Blacks and Indians, grew tired of the whites and their discriminatory ways. And just like the blacks and Indians, Mexicans could not vote or sit in on a jury. So in the 1950's a few smart spics with some legal know-how got together and decided to challenge the Gringo's law.

They took a high profile murder case, Texas vs. Hernandez to force the white man to categorize the Mexicans as Black, Indian or White. This made it all the way to the Texas Supreme Court where it was decided that Mexicans were considered legally white. However this confused the spics even more!

Their newly found category did not seem to impress anyone as they strutted around town like regular citizens. They wondered why they were not accepted and treated like White Folks. They still were looked down upon as second and third class citizens. Mistreatment of Mexicans was accepted and practiced throughout the southern states.

My family has a history in the Southwest dating back before 1818, when it was still under Spanish rule. My Great-Grandmother Maria Ochoa, who was born in Bisbee, Arizona, washed and ironed for the rich white man. In the 1820's Arizona became a part of Mexico. Then in 1912, Arizona became the forty-eighth state of this great country.

My great-grandmother went through three nationalities without ever having to move her rocking chair. This means she was first a Spaniard, then a Mexican, and finally an American. But guess what she'll always be called?

Yup...a Mexican!

My Grandmother and Grandfather, Inez and Vicente Elias, were born and raised in Arizona. In the early 1890's they purchased three lots in Tempe, Arizona. On these lots, they built two houses out of adobe bricks. As of today, these houses have been restored to their original state and are recorded in the National Registry of Historical Places. The house is now a museum and cultural center, symbolic of the roles Hispanics of Mexican-American ancestries contributed toward the building and development of the city of Tempe.

As I look at an old picture of my Grandma standing in her garden, I see a pioneer woman who carved out a piece of the old southwest for herself and her family. She and other Pioneers like her, not only had to deal with the native Indians but the influx of white European immigrants. The fact that Inez Elias was Hispanic, nullifies her as being presented or looked upon as a pioneer of American history.

Most articles and books written about America, and its beginnings, neglect to mention the Hispanic Contribution in building this great country. I bring this up because even in this day, in the new millennium, South Westerners are still considered foreigners or illegals - or both! Yet, on the eastern border of this nation, Caucasians stepping off a boat just arriving from Europe are automatically **visually** tagged as Americans.

Raised in the forties, in a multi-cultured neighborhood, I never considered or cared much about racial differences. Maybe it was because I was a kid, and kids don't get too hung up on such things. Racism usually doesn't kick in until we reach young adulthood. That's when the competition of life begins - Where all qualified contenders jockey for position at the starting gate in preparation for the big race. The starting positions are usually determined by one's color and ethnicity.

One thing I found odd as a youth was that there were no Asians in our school. The only Chinese people I knew owned and operated a vegetable market. Come to think of it, where were all the Japanese kids? How come no Japanese! I was too young to know that they were all in internment camps. Thinking back to that time, I realize there were no black people either, except for one black kid in my class - a pretty girl by the name of Beverly Smith.

Oh, and at the top of the hill where I lived there was a nice neat little town called City Terrace. The houses were built mostly in the Spanish tradition. This is where the rich Jewish people lived. Whenever us kids needed a few coins to go to the show, we would pick avocados from our trees and sell them two for a nickel to these rich folks. In those days, you could get into the movies for nine cents.

Speaking of the Jewish people brings to mind the Holocaust and what the Jewish people were put through by the White Nazis. But you know what? Jews are not alone when it comes to suffering greatly because of race. Whites, for various reasons, have spent a lot of time and energy incarcerating minorities into slave camps, concentration camps, internment camps, and reservations. The following is a list of examples of attempts to exterminate a race of people.

- **The near-extermination of the Native American Indian when the White Europeans first came to this country.**

- **The attempt by the White Nazis to exterminate the Jews.**

- **The system of apartheid against all nonwhite people in South Africa by Whites.**

- **The horrific treatment of the African Negros, who were captured, and imported to America by whites to be sold into slavery.**

- **The taking over by whites of the entire southwest geographically and financially from the early Spanish settlers. (Mexicans)**

And...Sometimes it was white against white!

During the depression, an anxiety prevailed over the shortage of jobs in California. There wasn't even enough work for the new white settlers. Adding to the problem was the influx of more white immigrants coming west seeking work. Surprisingly, these white job seekers weren't from another country but from a region in the Midwest - An area more commonly known, as the "Dust Bowl."

White Folks, fearing for their own existence, felt something had to be done about these new white immigrants saturating the state. So to protect California from this onslaught of job seekers, White citizens (Minute men) decided to take matters into their own hands as they put up their own check lines at the California border to prevent further white southerners from entering the state. They also denied entrance to Black immigrants who fled the south just because it was the south.

Another group singled out during the depression by these self proclaimed white protectors of California's population, was the Native Mexican Americans who were here when California was just a puppy. Whites took it upon themselves to load these lazy spics in trucks and ship them to a place distant and foreign to them. (Mexico) Not too much is ever mentioned about this part of California History.

The Japanese people have their own story to tell. On December 7th 1941, Japan attacked Pearl Harbor. And because of this terrible act, we were systematically programmed to believe that all Japanese people were evil. And for the sake of our homeland security, we rounded up all these Japanese American citizens and locked them up in interment camps. And just for good measure, we locked up their evil women and children too!

Their land and family holdings were confiscated with no knowledge or promise of what would become of them. These camps were located in different parts of the country. California, with its biggest population of Japanese had the most internment camps.

As a kid, I was taught by the media to believe that Japanese people were little ugly things who would slit your throat at the drop of a hat. And when it came to the women, they would first abuse them sexually – then slit their throat.

In those days it was politically correct and considered more enjoyably offensive to call them "Japs." Some of the older folks probably remember the early World War Two movies, where Japanese people were called "Nips," A name short for "Nippon," which was Japan's original name.

I had never seen or met a Japanese kid until I was in Junior High School. During my early childhood they had all been locked up with their folks somewhere in the desert in internments camps. When these Japanese kids were freed and allowed to do regular American things like enrolling in schools, I was more than surprised in meeting these new enrollees. I was confused at how different these new entrants to my Junior High School were compared to what I had been led to believe. They were not mean and cruel as advertised, but were the nicest, smartest, and best students in school. Their respect for their elders is something to be admired.

The Japanese people seem to have a genuine kindness and politeness for people of all races. One good example I could give you of a good and decent Japanese guy, is my dentist who spent his childhood in an internment camp. He sold his successful dentistry business to work with his son and daughter-in-law to do missionary work in the hell holes of the orient.

He joked about how he was only five years old when his family was freed from a camp located in one of the eastern states. He remembered his first big excitement on being released was seeing a town all lit up like a Christmas tree. He had never seen neon lights - He thought it was magic!

I'll always have the highest regard for my dentist who is one of the nicest, most charitable and wisest men I have ever had the pleasure of knowing. I thought it odd, and wondered why only the Japanese people were singled out to be interned in camps.

We were also at war with Germany and Italy - (Except for a few Germans and Italians who were sentenced to prison for espionage) How come none of them were ever interned? Maybe it was because Germans and Italians, with their European look, passed as traditional Americans.

Asian people, like the rest of us minorities, have always had a problem passing the American look test. We all look too foreign and not European enough! Even though some Asians have co-mingled with other cultures and races, most Asian people of today are still somewhat separated from mainstream America. They pretty well take care of themselves and their families. No winos or street people here!

In most cases the distinction between race and ethnicity (including Asians) has become blurred in time. Changes in skin color and physical appearance has weakened the once strong boundaries of the races. People have also mistaken religion, culture, or nationality as a race – as in the "Jewish Race" or the "Italian Race."

I myself, as a minority senior citizen, feel fortunate in living a good and healthy life amid a minimum amount of racism. Despite all that, and like most minorities, I too experience the subtleties of racism on a regular basis. Most minorities, through a lifetime of second class treatment, have a built in radar system for spotting racism. This includes the ability to understand racist tactics and code words - Something whites will never truly understand.

During the eighties, in visiting Atlanta, Georgia, my wife and I were surprised at how well the white and black people got along. I always thought there was still a lot of bad blood going on between those two races. Surprisingly, it was my wife and I that experienced a bit of insecurity as we felt ourselves being scrutinized.

I think Atlanta's confusion was that my wife and I (both East L.A. Mexicans) walked and talked among them as equals – We were actually gawked at like a foreign oddity. And the fact that we were clean and walking upright might have added to their dilemma.

Back home in L.A. while visiting my sister and her husband, the subject of our experience in Georgia came up. My wife and I told my sister and her husband, of how we were looked at strangely - by both blacks and whites. This made us feel a little uncomfortable.

I asked my sister, who is dark skinned and Mexican looking and her husband (who is of the Gringo persuasion) if they had ever experienced odd and questionable looks because of their differences. My sister and her husband, and without hesitation, answered simultaneously, but with contradicting answers. His was a definite "NO," while hers was a "Yes." It was funny to see their surprised reaction as they both stared at each other in disbelief. It was obvious he had never noticed looks out of the ordinary, while she on the other hand, was acutely aware of all the side glances. I found it oddly surprising that they had never discussed the subject.

My Gringo Brother-in-Law, a very nice guy and with who I have a wonderful relationship with, is typical of most whites and their belief that racism is almost nonexistent against minorities. And because of the mere fact that they don't belief racism exists, they never see it or recognize it whenever it does show its ugly head. Even when an act of racism is pointed out to them – they still don't get it! They've never had to experience the confusion and anxiety brought on when confronted by a racist – especially one in power.

Minorities on the other hand just to exist, have to live and breathe the stuff on a regular basis - To have to adapt to a life where they become comfortable as a compliant subservient.

One who accepts his or her second class status as a permanent way of life without change - To be able to wear a broad smile while extending a glad hand.

Because of these contradicting feelings between the races, history will continue to repeat itself - Unless of course, we as individuals mature to the level of complete equality – where minorities are no longer scarred by a life time of discrimination, and whites have out grown their self-proclaimed status of superiority.

Sounds like a lot to ask doesn't it? Yes it is a lot to ask! That's why I am constantly asking myself, God, and any other source of reliable information, "WHY?" Why does this unfair situation continue to exist where the white population own and have most of just about anything that is valuable - A life where some are definitely more fortunate than others? And how come they manage to stay in power so as to keep it that way. And most importantly how do we, as minorities, gain our fair share of lifes bounties.

And how do we convince these fortunate whites to play nice and share some of their goodies – Goodies that they originally acquired by hook or crook.

I've always wondered why we, as a society, continue to evolve to where we live longer, get bigger, healthier, and smarter – but never seem to get any better! I honestly believe that no one is really any better than anyone else.

And with that said, I do believe however, that some of us do have the delightful distinction of being more fortunate – such as being richer, smarter, taller and prettier – and of course, whiter!

BUT NONE ANY BETTER!

Maybe our next chapter entitled **"Who and what is a minority"** might answer a few of these questions.

Part Five

Who and what are
"Minorities"

The word "minority," in relation to race, is sometimes misleading - It lends to the idea that minorities are a mass of a lesser amount. On the contrary minorities, when grouped together, make up the bulk of a society.

I believe it all began when a group of restless people in search of greener pastures, wandered into another tribe's territory and set up camp. Because these newcomers looked different and did things a different way, they were not readily accepted into the new tribe. This negative treatment forced the immigrants to assimilate in segregated groups keeping mostly to themselves.

These clustered groups of lesser numbers were recognized and labeled as "Minorities." Webster defines Minority as the smaller number of a whole; opposed to majority.

We've come a long way from those early days when tribes consisted of people having the same culture, habits, and color. But since then, and with all the co-mingling that has gone on, we are now at a point in history where the line separating minorities is pretty well blurred. It's no more a strong division between white and black.

Historically, a minority's role on this planet has been one of poverty and struggle. Their reaction to leadership is usually that of subservience, or rebellion – depending on the leadership. Most of our great leaders, who have personally sacrificed for the betterment of others, have been minorities with a righteous cause.

While referring to the rest of us as Minorities, Whites prefer to think of themselves as the "Majority." The Los Angeles Times, on August 25, 2006, ran an article showing the ethnic transitional growth of the Southland dating back to the year nineteen seventy.

This article, based on a 2000 census with maps and a pie chart, revealed that Latinos with 45% of the population were now the majority. Does this mean as the Hispanic race is elevated to a majority position, do they automatically assume all the perks and ruling power that go with it? Does it also mean Whites, who are now the minority, have to give up the driver's seat! **I don't think so!**

Another article in the Los Angeles Daily News (Aug. 14, 08) gave us a peek at the racially diverse future of this country. In 2008, according to the U.S. census Bureau, one out of three Americans is a minority. It is projected that in 2042, minorities will be the majority.

The word "Minority," in reference to people, and no longer a number count, has evolved as a negative thing defining a group, or groups of people, as poor and less educated. Regardless of minority numbers, whites have established the fact that people of Asian, African, or Hispanic heritage are "Minorities."

Here's an example of how minorities are thought of by most whites. Newt Gingrich, ex-Speaker of the House, on Ted Koppel's "Nightline" declared, "Most crime is committed by Blacks, Hispanics, and some poor Whites." By his statement, Mr. Gingrich declares that all blacks and Hispanics are potential criminals, while only some poor whites, down on their luck, might commit a crime.

Speaking about "Minorities and their penchant for crime," when it comes to the ladder of success, minorities usually hang out on the bottom rung. This is due mainly to guys like Ol' Newt who have a mind-set that minorities who are unintelligent and less civil are indeed more capable of committing a crime.

Because of this continual existence as second class citizens minorities, as human beings, have felt a need and desire to improve their situation. And because of this need, along with certain negative circumstances, People of Color have been known to resort to crime. A Good deal of these crimes are committed out of necessity – Like to feed and house their families.

Unlike the poor guy who steals a loaf of bread to feed his family the crooks at the top level of society, steal purely out of greed. An article was written on the disparity of the difference in the justice system between minorities and white collar criminals. One out of every hundred citizens of the general population of the U.S. is in Jail. And of the Blacks, between the ages of 18-24, one out of nine is in jail. Minorities generally end up going to jail more often and do more time. It's also proven more money is taken through fraud and white collar crime than the street type. And they do less time – if any!

As this paragraph is being written, January 09, the headlines of the day are filled with the name "Madoff." This man Bernard Madoff is involved in the biggest heist in American history. He is accused, and has admitted to, a financial investment scam of 50 billion dollars. And yes, because of his color and the exorbitant amount of money involved, he is out on bail and residing in his lavish penthouse.

But while out on bail this Bernie guy thought he would be clever and hide his ill-got-gains by distributing some of it among his family. He was caught by the authorities and hauled back into court and was verbally reprimanded. He was again released and returned to his apartment. You'd think, a smart man like him, would've learned the first time. (Update: Bernie was eventually jailed for his crime)

The unfairness of the white ruling class, whether in business or the justice system, has always been unfavorable for minorities of all colors and cultures. Whitey, by nature, will always and automatically assume the position of the boss. And to maintain that position, he or she will do what ever it takes and be what ever they have to be to maintain that position - this leaves minorities with very little or no chance of ever becoming the boss. This is generally why you find them filling the jobs of servants and laborers.

The following is a good example of the white man boss and his relationship with minorities. This is a story told to me by a black co-worker who grew up in the south. He was raised during the thirties when discrimination was not only accepted but considered the white mans right. Simply walking down the road was a challenge for a black person. My friend remembers having to jump in a ditch whenever a white man would aim his car at him.

When it comes to dealing with the enemy (An uppity Nigger) Whites will usually unite to protect their superior status.

A BLACK BOY'S EXPERIENCE IN THE SOUTH

My first boss and friend in the entertainment business was a black southern gentleman from the Deep South. He told me how as a ten year old boy in the thirties living in Louisiana, he was physically thrown off the sidewalk by a couple of White men. The sidewalk, actually a boardwalk, was considered unofficially off limits to blacks. But when foot traffic was light, with no whites around, blacks would chance it and treat themselves to a stroll on the boardwalk.

One day my friend, as a ten year old, was in town to pick up a blue shirt he had ordered through a Catalog Company with money he had earned picking cotton. After admiring himself with his new shirt in the store mirror, and feeling proud and confident, he walked to the door and stepped out on the boardwalk.

The morning was quiet and the streets, besides being empty, were thick with mud. Seeing no one around, and not wanting to get his new shirt dirty, my young friend decided to treat himself to a walk on the exclusive boardwalk – just like a white man.

He was about halfway down the street when two White men, apparently involved in a heated argument, came bursting out of a doorway. The men were angry and close to blows when they spotted the young black boy up on the boardwalk. My friend figured the white men, engrossed in their fight, would ignore him and just let him walk on by. But no such luck!

The two men, immediately forgetting their dispute and coming together like blood brothers against a common foe, grabbed the ten year old boy and threw him into the muddy street. My friend picked himself up and looking at his new shirt covered with mud began to cry.

This story of my friend, and others like it, is where minorities first learn where they stand in the pecking order of man. It pretty well defines the priorities of the white man and his claim of superiority. Whether inherently or culturally induced most white people born and bred in the United States, while denying they are racist, honestly believe they are superior to people of color. (Minorities)

As an adult my friend, throughout his career, has had the same and continuous problem with the white man boss. When he was first hired back in the fifties at NBC as a "Paint Boy," he was told this would always be his job and not to expect anything more.

Coming from the poverty of the south where white folks had the only say, he accepted this permanent maintenance position graciously. After forty years as a maintenance worker with no chance of advancement, and who had trained and helped others to advance, he quietly retired. He passed away in 2008.

The sad part of it is most minorities do not argue the point believing that they are indeed inferior to Whites. This feeling of a lesser being is derived from having to live a life under a negative stereotypical portrayal. I must admit, I fit into this category.

As an individual, raised as a minority and influenced by the negatives of being a minority, I will never be able to shake the second-class feelings of insecurities so ingrained in my being. As a kid, I never considered myself a minority. All I knew was that there were all kinds of different people; some big- some small – some dark and some light - Oh, and then there were some with a lot more money than others.

This is the group I wanted to belong to – the money group! But once again, being a minority the odds of me amassing a lot of money aren't very good. I will always consciously, or unconsciously, consider myself a second-class citizen.

Being a minority in this country is like being handicapped; you're never considered or accepted as a whole individual. This makes it difficult to succeed in both leadership and business.

I've never pictured myself, or had the ambition of ever holding a position of authority – you know, being the boss! I always thought those jobs were for smart ambitious college guys. You know guys, who at a very young age were told how important it was to get a good education and be a success.

But now, as a veteran of corporate dealings, it has become more than apparent that having a white collar, clean fingernails, and an education do not make a good leader. In fact, more than likely, they are more apt to be a better follower - An individual that will go along with just about anything for chance at the gold ring.

The word success can have a whole lot of different meanings to people and their goals. Immediately, one goes for the obvious – Success means lot's of power and lot's money. With that kind of thinking, most of our great leaders would be considered failures. Gandhi, Mandela, Chavez, King, and even Mother Teresa who dedicated her life to helping the poor and hungry, never achieved great riches. I'm not even going to bring Jesus into this argument.

My personal goals were always very simple; keep character and dignity in tact while doing the very best I could. Honesty and fairness is always the first priority of the game. But judging by today's standards, those personal traits are not considered compulsory in making it to the top. Just look at the past few years and some of the jokers who've been screwing things up in both politics and big business.

As a retired Geezer, who's had a few run-ins with bosses, I've learned that the best leaders are those more concerned with the plight of others than their own ambitions. I know that sounds corny, but you know what? Corny will always trump selfish greed and bullshit!

This brings us to the next chapter - Leadership.

Part Six

Minorities in, or in opposition to

Leadership

Simply put, leadership is a position of guidance - A conductor of sorts - The principal and most influential Chief. Put 'um all together and they spell "Boss!" Now this is what it's all about! It starts with kids playing the all time favorite "King of the Hill," and continuing as grown-ups seeking to be "Numero Uno." Or like President George W. Bush liked to refer to himself as, "The Decider."

It's been said of the many ways greatness is acquired, three stand out as the most popular. One of the most popular of the three is those with an insatiable ambition for personal gain, who will try to achieve their goals by any means possible. Next is those deserving of greatness with a life time of merit and hard work. Lastly we have those, through special circumstance, have greatness thrust upon them.

Let's start with those who through circumstance, along with a lot of personal struggle and sacrifice, have immortalized themselves for the benefit of mankind.

 **Gandhi -** an East Indian born in 1869 - educated in law at the University College in London and was admitted to the British Bar. Working in Africa, under White British rule, a dark skinned Gandhi found himself treated as an inferior individual. Armed only with a shield of truth, he developed a following as he courageously and non-violently challenged the white rule in the struggle for the rights of Indians. Gandhi was assassinated in 1948.

 **Martin Luther King Jr.** – (1929-1968), American clergyman and Noble Prize winner was a principal leader in the American civil rights movement and a prominent advocate of nonviolent protest. King's challenge of segregation and racial discrimination in the 1950s and 1960s helped convince many white Americans to support the cause of civil rights in the United States. After his assassination in 1968, King became a symbol of protest in the struggle for racial justice. His legendary struggle and inspiring speeches have placed him on the list of greats.

"Individuals should be co-workers with God."
– Martin Luther King

 **Caesar Estrada Chavez** (1927-93) in 1962 helped form the National Farm Workers association, which later became the United Farm workers of America. Chavez, in his attempt to organize the powerless migrant farmworkers of California, personally sacrificed himself with hunger strikes. In 1968 he led a nationwide grape boycott which helped change the bargaining position of the California farmworkers. The success of his righteous stubborn position forced growers to provide better working conditions along with better wages.

One other individual I feel should be up there on that list of greats in creating an important positive change in a negative situation, is the humble but dedicated Rosa Parks. She chose to disobey the law by refusing to move to the rear of the bus by the request of a white person. Her act of defiance created a movement still in progress.

 **Rosa Parks,** In 1955, was arrested for disobeying a segregation law in Montgomery, Alabama - A law that required a black person to give up their seat on a bus whenever a white person requested it. Her action helped to stimulate a boycott where for over a year, blacks refused to use the city's bus system. This popular national boycott forced city officials to repeal the discriminatory law.

A similar story happened in the forties when a Black Army officer, while riding a bus in Texas, was asked to move to the rear of the bus. Dressed in uniform, the officer refused the request which led to his arrest and confinement for his defiance of the law. This lawbreaking Patriot later became the first Negro to break the color line in professional baseball. He was none other than Jackie Robinson.

 **Nelson Mandela,** in 1994, was the first black man ever elected president of South Africa. Prior to being elected, much of his life was spent in prison for leading black opposition to the oppressive white ruling Government. During his many years in captivity, Mandela became a world wide symbol of resistance to white domination in South Africa.

 **Mother Teresa** (1910-1997) was born Agnes Gonxha Bojaxhiu to Albanian parents in Skopje, which at that time was under the rule of the Ottoman Empire. At age 18 she entered the Order of our Sisters of the Lady of Loreto in Ireland. As principal of a Roman Catholic high school in Calcutta, Mother Teresa was moved by the presence of the sick and dying on the city streets. In 1948 she was granted permission to leave her post at the convent and begin a ministry for the sick and poor.

One story of Mother Teresa that comes to mind is a good example of what pure unselfishness and compassion for others is all about. While visiting the USA, Mother Teresa was invited to attend a Dinner hosted by President Ronald Reagan and his administration. She was picked up in a limo and delivered to the elegant hall where the big event was to occur. On her arrival, she was taken aback by the grandeur and the lavish feast prepared in her honor.

She politely refused their invitation saying, "With so much poverty and hunger through out the world, she could not in all that is right attend such an opulent affair." The red faced Reagan Administration quickly came up with a solution where if she attended the dinner, they would contribute the cost of the dinner ($100,000) to her ministry for the poor. Mother Teresa accepted the contribution.

 **Jesus Christ (0-33) born** in Bethlehem under unusual (and some say unbelievable) circumstances, is known to believers as the son of God - and according to non-believers, he was just another guy! Jesus was raised in Nazareth, Israel, a geographical area composed mostly of a darker skinned populous. Jesus is primarily known as rising from the dead after the ultimate sacrifice of giving his life for the sins of others. (A true photograph of Jesus could not be found so I used the image on the shroud of Turin)

Jesus was probably more Israeli looking than what we've been led to believe. I'd say he probably identified more with the darker hued Ben Kingsley of Gandhi fame, than the blond blue eyed Jeffery Hunter who portrayed Jesus in the movie "King of Kings." It's almost like everything has to be sanitized with an American look before entering this country.

Unlike most leaders of today none of these notables just mentioned ever sought personal position, fame or riches. Their goal was that of a higher calling; to mend, fix, or alter conditions detrimental to a society and its people. For their unselfish contributions to mankind, and instead of material gains as a reward, they have become historical heroes in our, hearts, books, and minds. At last mention, Mother Teresa was headed for sainthood.

As God, or fate, has seen fit to send us individuals blessed with the foresight, compassion, and courage to set us on a new course, God, by this same rule and to keep life in balance, has also periodically (and much too often) seen fit to saddle us with greedy, self serving, egotistical leaders sick enough to bring harm to their country and its people. This brings us to the other option of seeking position by unethical and dastardly deeds.

 One bad guy that jumps off the page, and is considered to be one of the most evil dictators in history, is none other than "Adolph Hitler." When it comes to racism, and prejudice against a group or groups of people, he tops the list. How did this little guy amass so much evil power? And why did the people allow it? The timing in history must have been just right for this guy. Along with a group of his evil cohorts, he almost accomplished what he set out to do – **Rule the world!**

Hitler is one example in a field of many. What a shame that God, or fate, doesn't simply keep life fair and balanced with an equal amount of good and evil leaders. Instead, history has proven there are a lot more not-so-good leaders than good ones.

Maybe there's some reason God challenges us with a lot of heavies – He wants to see what we do about it. Do we allow these unscrupulous leaders to entice us with the carrot of success, or do we stand tall and take an ethical uncompromising position?

Since the beginning of time this world has had its share of corrupt leaders with an obsession for power and riches. These go-getters come in all colors and levels of evil. When it comes to us humans, our behavior has always been in question.

Simply put, most of us are as good as we have to be, and as bad as we are allowed to be. Just ask any unsupervised kid. And when we're exposed to the temptation of power, this is where rules and laws become invalid to the weaker of us.

In fact, ethics and regulations are nothing but road bumps for those of questionable motives on their way to the top. Just ask any CEO or politician. And look at how God tested his own kid! Instead of giving him a position with the power to make all things right and good, he put him up to ridicule and merciless beatings - eventually leading up to his own crucifixion. Go figure!

Personally, I never did care about politics and who was in power. To me politics was dull and boring. You know, where government organizations are so well managed by competent political nerds that no one really gets overly excited about it - except maybe on Election Day.

As a young man, all I knew or cared about politics was that Eisenhower was the president and everything was honky-dory. Jobs were easy to find, homes were easy to buy, and you could get gas and cigarettes for about two bits. All around, Life was pretty good...

"This was the fabulous fifties!"

Then in the sixties, along came a guy by the name of Richard M. Nixon who wanted to be president. To me, he spelled trouble from the beginning. This is where I decided to sit up straight and pay attention to who was driving the bus. There was something about this guy that yelled out "bad news." Like Nixon's eyes for instance, they never seemed to smile - no matter what the rest o his face was doing. There are certain guys who can laugh, smile, and grin without ever showing any emotion in their eyes. Kinda like George Bush!

Nixon's opponent for the presidency was **John F. Kennedy,** a guy I had never heard of. All I knew about him was that he was a rich Irish Catholic Dude who seemed to sincerely care about the average guy. And you know what - And just like the song "When Irish eyes are smiling" Kennedy's Irish eyes were always smiling! Well I voted for the guy and he won!

Kennedy, who contributed greatly to making this nation feel as one again, is considered to be one of our greater presidents. He and his wife Jackie, in touring other countries, were loved and hailed through out the world. But for some reason, beyond our understanding, he was taken away by the dastardly deed of an assassin by the name of Lee Harvey Oswald. He was shot in an open car while visiting Texas. To this day his assassination is still being debated by some.

One big reason we have such a history of bad leadership is that "good" people generally do not seek positions of power. This leaves the door wide open for unscrupulous ambitious types to walk right in.

Like for instance, the guy we were just talking about...

 **Richard Millhouse Nixon,** a devious man who was able to worm his way into the highest office of the land. Surprisingly, and under the cloud of "Watergate" (an illegal covert operation designed to undermine the Democratic Party) he was voted into office for a second term. Nixon's gang was found guilty of withholding evidence and obstructing justice by a congressional investigation. They were charged, convicted and jailed for their crimes. Vice President, Spiro Agnew, resigned under an investigation of corruption. Nixon, realizing he was about to be impeached, resigned in disgrace.

 Twenty years later, in the eighties, we had **Ronald Reagan** - another man who dealt in secrecy. He too, while under a suspicious controversy involving Iran and the Contranistas, (Iran-Contra) was elected for a second term in office. And once again, we had a congressional investigation of the president and his cabinet. Reagan got off claiming "Plausible Deniability."

Reagan's Vice President, George H. Bush, excused himself with, "I was out of the loop." However most, if not all, of the members of Reagan's Cabinet were charged and indicted for various crimes against the government. I believe Reagan still holds the record with the most indicted cabinet members. - A cabinet he personally selected.

 Ironically, with the passing of another 20 years in the year 2000, George W. Bush, the son of George H.W. Bush was selected into office. I say selected, because a controversial vote count left the decision up to George's Supreme Court buddies. Also ironically, and under a cloud of suspicion concerning the reasons for invading Iraq, Bush in 2004 was elected for a second term. We were hoodwinked into believing Saddam Hussein was involved in the attack on 911, and that his weapons of mass destruction were about to destroy us.

As this paragraph is being written (S' 2008), President Bush is into his last year of office with the lowest approval rating of any president. With a republican majority in the house and senate, Bush and his pals did just about anything and everything they wanted to. This resulted in creating a political national mess sending this country into a financial and moral tailspin.

A debate has been offered as to whether George W. Bush is considered to be one of the worst, if not the worst, presidents this country has ever seen. He also is considered a contender for beating Ronald Reagan's record for the distinction of picking out the worst cabinet. This argument also includes his shifty eyed Vice President Cheney who to this day (March 2010) is still spreading his lies about the invasion of Iraq. More of the Bush team, **Check it out!**

- Karl Rove, Bush's Chief Council and advisor, was said to be the chief architect for getting Bush elected. He had to resign amid questionable political controversies.

- Vice President, Dick Cheney, because of his controversial political ethics is the most unpopular VP - Ever! As a powerful and influential Vice President, he kept a low political profile.

- Cheney's Chief Council Scooter Libby, was tried and convicted of obstructing justice and lying to Congress. *Scooter Libby, close friend and confident of Cheney and Bush, had his sentence commuted by the President.*

- Carl Rumsfeld, Secretary of Defense had to resign due to complaints of his incompetence in running the war.

- Condoleezza Rice, National Secretary Advisor, because of her friendship and allegiance to the President was elevated to Secretary of Defense in Rumsfeld's departure.

- Paul Wolfewitz, Deputy Defense Secretary, also left under questionable circumstances.

- Colin Powell, Secretary of State, embarrassed by the Bush administration eventually resigned.

- Alberto Gonzalez, Attorney General and close (too close) friend of Bush also resigned under investigative pressure.

These are just a few among many loyal Bushies responsible for turning a rich and well respected country into a poor and hated one. If Speaker of the House, Nancy Pelosi, hadn't taking impeachment off the table, Mr. Bush would've gone through a congressional investigation just like Nixon and Reagan.

The reason for getting off the main subject of minorities is I wanted to lay the ground work for the unprecedented 2008 election where we had the first "ever" African American run for the office of the President of the United States of America.

Barack Hussein Obama – Who would'a thunk it!

Much has been said of this Harvard-trained lawyer turned Senator from Illinois. His Striking presence with a **"golden"** hue and winning smile along with a flare for public speaking has created quite a stir among the citizens of the good ol' USA. His color, derived from a black and white mixture, is evident in most political conversations - Some of it good, and some of it bad. AND, some of it kinda racist!

Unlike the rest of the world where the color of an individual is not a factor, a light-skinned person of dark ancestry in this country is considered and deemed 100% Black - And, in no way is this person allowed to assimilate his or her culture with the color white!

As mentioned earlier, intermixing of races was a no-no backed by a law originally designed in America to keep the White race pure. Many states defined a person with one fraction of black blood in them as Black. So if a white person was found to stray, their siblings were ostracized from the white race and demoted into the Black race.

It was also maintained that having one black great-grandparent was sufficient in defining a person as Black, but having seven white great-grandparents was not enough to make a person white. To further the white cause of superiority, it was proven scientifically by a group of white scientist (?) that Black people were considered to be only five-eighths of a human person.

This goes to show'ya that some races are culturally and socially constructed, and not always biological. It's pretty evident, who masterminded the construction of these races in America and why! Minority races were purposely designed by the ruling white class to lock people of color in a state of a second class citizenry.

But enough is enough! It's time we tear down that big racist wall built by whites to isolate themselves from the rest of us. It's been going on too long! We've got more and more citizens with a color resembling Barrack Obama than we do guys that look like "Dick Cheney." So with Obama's beautiful mix of half white and half black, he should be the poster boy for the new **"Golden Race!"**

Barack Obama's first big challenge in the 2008 presidential race came in the shape of a White European American woman by the name of Hillary Clinton. This was big - A Blackman and a White woman both vying for the nomination to represent the Democratic Party in a National Presidential Election.

This was the first time a White European woman had a serious shot for the office of the presidency. This was also a big plus for women's lib and for all women of European ancestry. Hillary was also considered clean, articulate, and a credit to her race.

You know what? I just found out my computer won't accept "Whitewoman," as one word. Yet!!! In writing the word Black man, I could type it either way; Blackman or Black man. Seee!!! Umm…I wonder if it will accept "Blackboy" as one word. Nope, the computer wouldn't accept that either. It kept coming up underlined in red.

Anyway, in this unprecedented contest for the highest office of the land, Hillary Clinton was simply referred to as a female candidate, whereas Barack Obama was continually introduced as an African American. Now that he's a candidate, shouldn't he be considered and accepted as just a plain old American…like Hillary?

And what if he wins the presidency; do we call him our African American President? - Or, our Black President? - Or how about "The skinny kid with the funny name!" That's what he called himself during the 2004 democratic convention. And could you imagine if Hillary had to carry around the label of Arian, Anglo, or European American? I don't think so!

How come we folks of color have to carry our ethnicity around with us as a tag - making us always sound like "Foreign Americans?"

Despite his educational and practical experience in the race for the democratic nomination, Barrack Hussein Obama was considered by his competition as young and inexperienced. In contrast, his opponent, Hillary Clinton claimed to be experienced enough to take over as Commander in Chief on day "ONE" – and at three in the morning!

The campaigning for the nomination of the Democratic Party turned out to be a hot contested race with a lot of mud slinging. One big positive for Obama, which was considered a negative by both McCain and Hillary, was his Rock Star presence with a flare for public speaking.

His speaking ability created quite a stir in both Hillary and McCain as it displayed their contempt for Barack's popularity. McCain expressed his disdain for Obama by saying, "All he can do is give a good speech." Hillary went a little further by adding, "All he does is fill a hall or stadium with a lot of cheering fans."

Hillary was a passionate and formidable contender in her quest for the White House. She even resorted to making up stories about her duties as first lady. One big whopper was when landing in a battle ridden country; she said she had to duck and run to avoid the sniper fire cracking over head. An actual photo of that landing showed her smiling as she and other arrivals walked across the landing strip.

Despite her good showing in winning a lot of the primaries, Hillary came in second to Obama, and under pressure from her fellow democrats reluctantly conceded the race. She was told she would hurt the party if she continued to run.

Her disappointment in not winning and having to give in to Obama was obvious as she took her loss very hard. She claimed the reason for her loss was that the media was unfairly sexist. She finally, and again under pressure from her fellow Senators, reluctantly came around by endorsing Obama as the democratic candidate for the office of the Presidency.

Her husband Bill Clinton, former President (1992-2000) was also visibly upset at her loss. It appeared at times, as he campaigned for Hillary, that he was running for the democratic nomination. Bill, at one time, was endeared by most Blacks - In fact, during Bills day, Blacks jokingly referred to Bill Clinton as the first Black President.

During his campaigning for his wife Hillary, Bill's passionate criticism of Obama caused some to accuse him of being a racist. He publicly responded to the charges of racism by his customary manner of lowering his head, pointing his finger at the camera, and while peeking out through the top of his eyes claim, **"I am not a racist!"**

Bill, a product of his southern culture, will never consider himself a racist - And like most southerners, have no idea how racist they really are. But in defense of these crackers, most of them do have a tender spot in their heart for blacks and their plight for equality.

That is until a serious competition between races pops up – you know, like a presidential race. This is where the white fangs come out!

I would say most of us, have a tender heart for the poor and less fortunate - but by our nature, we tend to envy those that are prettier, smarter, and richer than us. And if we had the choice between pity and envy, most of us would prefer a situation of feeling sorry for someone as opposed to being envious of them.

Bill Clinton was also asked repeatedly, and in many ways, if he thought Barack Obama was ready to be the next president. Back to his customary way of peeking out of the top of his eyes he replied, "No one is actually ready to be president." This came as a surprise for he had stated earlier that not only his wife Hillary was qualified for the presidency, but so were the other contenders. (All white)

Now Bill is basically a good man, and besides being caught with his pants down, was a good president. But like so many other whites he **"just can't help it."** Could you imagine if Barack Obama had won the presidency with Hillary as his VP? - And, could you also imagine, Barack in the drivers seat with Hillary besides him riding shotgun - and her husband sitting quietly in the rumble seat? I don't think so!

Bill is not alone in his endeavor to prove he's not a racist. Since "Political Correctness" has come on the scene, he's had plenty of company in the racial blunder line. With racist innuendos getting a lot of attention, the phrase **"I am not a racist"** has become rather common among Government Representatives and entertainers.

I say "Bullshit"... we're all racist! And whether we accept it or deny it, we are all prejudice to some degree! I for one have a thing for tall, pretty, rich people! And that's not just because I'm short, fat, poor, and Mexican. It's just the way it is! It's like claiming to be completely honest, when we know there is no such thing!

Here's a good one! While campaigning for the office of the presidency, Senator George Allen of Alabama committed a doosie of a faux pas. It happened outdoors while addressing a crowd of admirers. Allen spotted a dark skinned individual in the crowd and laughingly pointed to the darkie calling him "Macaque" - A word of African origin taken to mean "Monkey."

Unfortunately for Senator Allen, a cell-phone reporter caught the incident on tape and made it embarrassingly public for him. Allen, realizing his political future was at stake, immediately went into a denial mode claiming "I am not a racist!"

He also said he had no idea what the word macaque meant. You'd think the Senator, being a Senator, could've come up with something that was not quite so lame.

It was soon disclosed that Senator Allen had been caught in a big whopper and was well aware of the word macaque and its meaning. Allen, who is proud of his southern heritage, also had some interesting nick-knacks in his office - Like for instance, an old hanging noose which was originally used for lynching blacks. Needless to say, his ambition for the office of the presidency was put on hold. But guys like him always manage to return.

Another example of a white guy putting his foot in his mouth was when Joe Biden first heard of Barack Obama, he described the African American as "clean and articulate." I'm sure Biden was sincere in his observation of Obama, and honestly believed he was being complimentary of the young man.

However nice the compliment was meant to be, would Joe have ever said the same thing about one of his political white brothers? I don't think so! Ironically, Barack Obama in his search for a running mate decided on picking Joe as his vice-president. This to me puts Obama way below the norm of prejudice.

Another off-the-wall compliment was when Bill O'Reilly, Fox News Network commentator after attending a luncheon in Harlem, reported how nice and normal blacks behaved in a restaurant. How they all ate quietly and were so well mannered. Bill said he never even heard one black customer yell out, "Hey, I want some mother f---ing tea." Bill's response when confronted was the customary, "I'm not a racist." I'm sure Bill thought he too was being complimentary to Blacks.

The sad part of O'Reilly and Biden is that they are not aware of their racial problem. Not even a little bit! Hell, they can't help it…they just don't know any better! As young'ns they were taught to believe that people of color really are inferior. O'Reilly has publicly declared, "There are no racist in this country!"

Another major public **faux pas** was when Don Imus, radio and TV personality on MSNBC, in discussing the Rutgers College girl's basketball team, used a derogatory term in describing them. Imus, in a jovial manner, called the almost all black champion girls team "Nappy Headed Hos."

Political activists Reverend Jessie Jackson and Reverend Al Sharpton publicly voiced their objections to Imus' remark and called for his **immediate dismissal.**

Imus, unaware of his racial blunder, skated for a few days before he realized his comment had become a hot media topic. The two reverends, Sharpton and Jackson, were also outraged that the general populace was slow in recognizing this racial remark as offensive.

In a televised press conference, the black female coach of the girl's team spoke eloquently in denouncing Imus's words. It was almost a week before any opposition to the derogatory remark finally surfaced forcing Imus to make a public apology to the girls which they gracefully accepted. Imus was soon let go by NBC, and because of his high ratings, was quickly picked up by CBS.

In August, 07, Jim Anderson of CNN did a special on Imus and his ordeal with the networks. Imus' problem was discussed by members of an all white panel of "experts" on the subject of racism. This has always amazed me, that people who have no idea of what racism is; feel they can judge who and what is a racist.

Another incident that cost someone their job was when "Al Campanis, General Manager of the Los Angeles Dodgers, was asked "Why aren't there any Black managers in baseball." His answer was typical for a white man, "They do not have the capabilities to manage a team." Translation: "They're too dumb to run things!"

One more quickie on public racial gaffs; Michael Richards (Cramer) of "Seinfeld" fame, while doing one of his comedy stage routines, called a black heckler in the audience a "Nigger." This too drew a bit of excitement, causing quite a media frenzy. And, once again we were subjected to the customary **"I am not a racist!"**

Funny though…in their veiled attempt to disguise who they truly are and what they really believe, their true side eventually pops up in a racial gaff. Luckily, we have plenty of minorities around to remind them of their racist side.

Wow, I've gotten way off the subject here! I'd better get back to Barack and politics. I found it interesting to hear political news commentators, in reference to Whites, use the phrase "Middle Class Blue Collar Americans." It was also amusing when these same white pundits would go back and correct themselves by inserting the words, **"Hard working."** Funny, how that term "hard working" is never inferred in reference to minorities.

The news guys and pundits could never understand why Barack had such a hard time in the polls getting acceptance of these so called "Hard working blue collar middle class Americans." Isn't that just a fancy code phrase for, "White Racist?"

It was interesting observing these same pundits bite their lip and squirm in their seats as they tried in vain to sincerely praise the achievements of this struggling young black in this unprecedented race for the White house.

Regardless of how disguised the bias was from the white media, there was always a strong undercurrent of racism hidden between the lines. Considering where these crackers come from, and what they have been programmed to believe, their behavior is understandable.

Then there's the problem of Barracks middle name "Hussein," which to some automatically means "Muslin." – And in this country, Muslin is considered a bad thing usually associated with terrorism. The controversy of Barack's middle name was quite a hot topic. It created a controversy among national and local talk shows. One such person on the TV pulpit got a little ridiculous in making sure he used the name "Hussein" as often and as negative as he could.

During the Democratic Convention of Aug. 2008, Chris Matthews of MSNBC's "Hardball" was confronted by a lady who stated Barack Obama was registered Muslin. She presented herself as part of a credible election group. With further questioning from Chris, the lady's credibility soon fell apart.

Chris was rather upset at the lady as he finished with, "She didn't care if Obama was Muslin or not, she just wanted to spread the false message by getting her story out."

This reminds me of that terrorist kid Tim McVeigh from Oklahoma who blew up a government building. When I first heard the news on the radio, one of the announcers automatically assumed it was done by an Arab Muslin. He said, "We must catch the dirty Muslin terrorist before he leaves the country." Then the announcer added, "Even if we don't get the right Muslin, we have to send those Arab terrorist a message." This also didn't seem to get much media ink, or air time.

Anyway, back to Senator Barack Obama and his win over Hillary as the Democratic nominee. His next big challenge for the White House was the Republican candidate John McCain, a rich white guy from the right side of the tracks. John's interesting resume included 26 years in the Senate, and 22 years in the Navy.

As a Naval pilot during the Vietnam War, John was shot down and captured. Because of this, he is considered a war hero. McCain, unlike most war veterans, is not shy about talking about the story of his incarceration in the Hanoi Hilton, where he was beaten and tortured for five years. Just ask him – he'll gladly show you his scars.

McCain admits as a young man he did it all! He was known as a boozer and a womanizer. One close friend of his called him a serial adulterer. He was still married to his first wife when he met and courted his present wife Cindy. In fact the ink was still wet on his divorce papers when John married Cindy. With all the negatives going on in McCain's past, his exploits never seemed to get much attention. How the heck do you pick on a white war hero?

Barack Obama, on the other hand, had a lot of pluses on his side. He is happily married to his first and only love Michele, and they have two daughters. He had a poor upbringing - nothing like the success and riches of the McCain family. He was raised by a single mom and grandma; he graduated from Yale with honors, and is now a Senator from Illinois. But the fact that he is "Half Black" automatically diminishes his achievements and qualifications.

During his campaigning, though being half white, Obama was always looked upon and addressed as Black. It was never mentioned outright, but his blackness was the most obvious of what some considered a negative. Realizing the big elephant in the political room, Obama put a well needed spotlight on Racism by way of an elegant and articulate speech on the subject. What he had to say on the subject was well praised and accepted by most Americans.

However, his personal appearance at such a high level on the political scene did bring out a few nagging questions by cynics:

- "Is he black enough?"
- "Is he too black?"
- "Is he American enough
- "Dose he have good American values?
- "When is he going to use his white side?"

McCain and his VP choice Sarah Palin, besides using the argument **"Is Barack Obama American enough,"** spent much, if not all, of their campaigning time trying to tarnish and diminish Obama's character. As they campaigned in some areas of what McCain and Palin described as real America, the crowds got pretty fired up over the Obama Anti-American rhetoric. In some areas of this beautiful country, the crowds spewed out hateful chants of "Muslin, Arab, and Terrorist." And besides the ol' standby of "Nigger," a few Yah-Hoos shouted out, "Kill Him."

Why didn't John McCain and Sara Palin put a stop to the hate mongers? Was it because they were too busy encouraging the rabid jeering crowds. On the flip side, whenever Barack Obama heard boos from his audiences, he'd tell them not to boo, but to **vote.**

During one of McCain's campaign speeches, in small town America, a lady claimed that Barack Obama was an "Arab." McCain quickly retrieved the microphone from the lady with this correction, "No…No, He's not that, he's a decent Man."

So, according to McCain, Arabs are not decent people - Not like us Americans anyway! I was not too surprised with McCain's response to what the nice lady from "White Middle America" had to say. The more I thought about McCain's answer, the more I thought to myself, "Why didn't McCain take a minute to educate the lady by telling her, Obama is not an Arab, he's an American, just like you and I."

But for some reason, and like most of Middle America, McCain and Palin have a hard time associating Barack Obama with the word American. Now why is that? Is it so ingrained in the heads of whites, that only they have the sole right to the title American.

Colin Powell, on "Meet the Press," said, "It goes further than simply denying Barack Obama is not an Arab, but a decent man!" Mr. Powell added, "Barack is not an Arab; he's a Christian - and what if Barack was not a Christian, but an Arab? Would that be such a bad thing in this land of the free, and home of the brave? This is not what this country is all about."

This article was inspired by Rep. Michele Bachmann of Minnesota who was very concerned about Obama's Anti-American views."

An American president

Patriotism isn't confined to one party or one candidate. To assert otherwise carries grave risks.

S THE PRESIDENTIAL campaign wends through its final days, a disturbing, discordant note has entered the vernacular of the race. After months of a spirited but serious debate about the future of the country — about whether our common lot is best safeguarded and advanced by a thoughtful young senator from Illinois or a tough veteran from Arizona — we now are hearing one side question whether the other is genuinely American.

Sarah Palin, in extolling the virtues of small towns, has mused about how they are "pro-America," presumably as distinct from the anti-American parts of the nation. Even more baldly, Republican Rep. Michele Bachmann of Minnesota told MSNBC that she was "very concerned" that Barack Obama "may have anti-American views." Although Bachmann declined interviewer Chris Matthews' invitation to name other members of Congress who were anti-American, she ventured the opinion that the American people would welcome an expose on those members who fit the bill. She later tried to extricate herself from her own mudslinging, but her previous comments were neither forced nor misconstrued.

Setting aside the amusing spectacle of a member of Congress calling on the media to expose members of Congress (careful what you wish for, congresswoman), it is worth considering the implications of this alleged anti-Americanism. We begin with what we hope is obvious to all: There is a difference between disagreeing about how to improve this country and asserting that one side of the debate is pro-America and the other is anti-America. Honest people can and do favor John McCain's tax policy or Obama's approach to the economy; thoughtful women and men, Americans all, prefer Obama on the environment or McCain on Iraq. Many Americans believe that Joe Biden is a w⸺ Palin is woefully unprepe⸺ Those are expressio⸺

country. Surely, though, it cannot be evidence of anti-Americanism when a person wants to become an American.

These new entries in the lexicon of patriotism represent a return to an era most of us hoped was consigned to history — when disagreement over policy became synonymous with disloyalty, when supporters of Social Security or Medicare were branded socialists, when those who believed in the rights of speech or association were considered radicals. Many of those who argued for their beliefs lost jobs; some went to prison.

Indeed, it is within the living memory of many of those who will vote next week that Americans were divided into the patriotic and the "un-American." The latter made up a large group with vague contours, from spies for the Soviet Union to conscientious protesters whose words or actions penetrated the alcoholic haze of Sen. Joseph McCarthy.

The investigations of that Red Scare era did yield some disloyal citizens. It is now largely accepted, for instance, that Julius Rosenberg was a Soviet spy. But the revelations of genuine threats to national security were small next to the damage done by the Red-baiters. McCarthy and his colleagues smeared high officials and low-level government workers, dentists, teachers, writers, actors, lawyers, college presidents. They cowed others into silence with the threat of public pillory. In the words of the Supreme Court, they engaged not in legitimate inquiry but in the exercise of intimidation, yielding to the desire to "expose for the sake of exposure."

We are not at that tragic stage today. But it is worth remembering that much travesty preceded McCarthy's tragedy. His ability to wound was aided by the acquiescence of many who knew better. One man who studiously refused to challenge McCarthy was President Eisenhower; he declined to confront him directly in order to deny the senator a place on the presidential stage. In the end, McCarthy was censur⸺ Senate and died not long after fered in the inter⸺ equately ⸺ car⸺

Ripped from the L.A Times Editorial Section – Oct. 26, 2008

131

In this unprecedented race for the presidency most good Americans, regardless of color, are concerned about the safety of Mr. Obama. History reminds us of how blacks have been threatened whenever they've approached the white sanctity of a white boundary or record.

It's understandable, yet not acceptable, why whites in their struggle to maintain their position of superiority in all aspects of life, while praising God and his blessings, continue to behave in a selfish and greedy manner. They've proven their unwillingness to give up any perks and advantages they enjoy just for being white. Their basic unyielding feeling must be, "The end justifies the means."

On this date of September 11, 2008 (The anniversary of 9-11) while campaigning for the presidency, Barack Obama in reference to John McCain's economic program, used the phrase "If you put lipstick on a pig, it's still a pig." It was obvious to anyone with a third grade education that Obama was in no way calling Sarah Palin a pig.

John McCain and his campaign staff were outraged that Barack would use those words in his campaign speech. They twisted Barack's meaning to appear insulting to McCain's choice for VP Sara Palin. The media was also quick to jump all over this as they ran the distasteful comment day and night.

However, when it was later disclosed that McCain had used the same phrase, word for word in eight various speeches throughout the years, he was not given nearly the amount of negative air time that Barack got. **There's definitely a double standard when it comes to the importance of who said what and when.**

This double standard has also become evident in the candidate's personal lives, which Include religion, friends and business associates. Barack Obama and his wife Michelle have both been put under a serious microscope. Barack has admitted to experimenting with drugs in his youth. He also was given forty lashes for his relationship with the Rev. Wright who dammed America for the treatment of blacks. In Wright's defense, he was a victim of the riotous sixties - police brutality and all! I'm sure he felt he had reason to spew hatred for a country that allowed citizens to legally abuse blacks as they attempted to assimilate into a white society.

And Michelle, Obama's wife, was also strapped to the yardarm for claiming, "She was finally "really" proud to be an American." Her words were configured in ways to portray her as an individual not proud of her country. When questioned about her patriotism, she responded simply with, "I am really proud of the possibility that a black man could truly have a shot at being the President.

McCain's wife Cindy, jumped all over Michelle Obama's "finally proud to be an American" statement as un-American. Cindy professed her own patriotism by immediately claiming she has always been proud to be an American. Surprise, Surprise! Can you believe it? An ultra rich WHITE LADY who loves being an American - Even if it took a few drugs to help her make it through the not-so-proud times.

I'd like to ask Cindy and her likes if they were proud of this country when they systematically took this land from the Indians – imported Africans to be used as slaves – used and abused the early Hispanic settlers in the South West – And, how about the forties when Japanese Americans were incarcerated because of Pearl harbor.

And let us not forget the sixties when segregation was introduced in the South and the abuse on blacks not only continued, but escalated. I guess this never affected the Cindy's of the world who never have suffered from racial hatred. Then there's Mr. McCain who, while as a prisoner of war and subjected to torturous treatment, finally realized his love of country. You mean, this rich white guy who has enjoyed all the perks this country has had to offer, never truly loved his country until his ordeal in Vietnam? Funny, how McCain's late realization of his love of country never did get any air time - Nothing close to Michelle's claim of finally being proud of her country.

And how about those opinion polls that are supposed to predict how candidates are doing in a political race. Some of these polls are cleverly written and purposely disguised to achieve certain results. This is further proof of how racist some of us really are. Could you imagine what the results of those polls would've been if the situation were reversed? If McCain (with the same qualifications) was Black and Obama (also with the same qualifications) was white? Whoa…mind boggling isn't it.

Speaking of polls brings to mind back in the day when the Mayor of Los Angeles, Tom Bradley, decided to run for the office of Governor of California. Tom had exhausted his terms as Mayor of Los Angeles, and was a heavy favorite to win the Governor's spot. And although way ahead in the polls, come Election Day, lo, and behold, he lost to a white guy.

It was then determined that citizens, when asked by pollsters if they had a problem voting for a Blackman, were not too honest in their replies. It's not that surprising to most People of Color, that whites feel more comfortable with one of their own. This proves that color is a **big** factor to an individual's decision when selecting a candidate in the confines of a voting booth. This experience of an upset in the California election is now known as the "Bradley Effect" theory.

There is so much more I could write on Politics, especially in today's presidential race. On this day, October 30, 2008 - five days before this Obama/McCain election, and as mentioned earlier, this race is hotly contested with all kinds of mud slinging going on. Barack Obama appears to be taking the high road, while John McCain, who is behind in the polls, is more or less pulling out all the stops.

I get my daily political fix from the TV - CNN, MSNBC, C-SPAN and sometimes a little bit of the FOX channel – and that's just for contrast and laughs! On the radio, I listen to Air America. And again for contrast and laughs, I'll turn on Limbaugh, or Hennessey.

Besides radio and TV, I try to read a couple of newspapers a day. There was a Los Angeles columnist by the name of Robert Sheer who I thought did a great job of keeping us all aware of President Bush's questionable leadership due to his incompetence. But because of Sheer's outspokenness he no longer writes for the L.A. Times.

Come to think of it, there have been others who have been shut out of the system for speaking truth to power. Phil Donahugh was one. He had a popular TV show on MSNBC which he used as a format to spread the word about Bush's lies. He was let go with the excuse that his ratings were low. (This was proven to be a lie)

Then Came the Dixie Chicks…Remember them? They were the singing group that, while on tour, publicly declared their dislike for President Bush. The President, along with his base of ditto-heads, denounced the girls for speaking up against him. In fact, Bush's basic philosophy was, "If you're not for me, you're for the terrorists."

Cyndi Sheehan was another one on Bush's list of unpatriotic trouble makers. She lost a son fighting in a war that Bush illegally started when he ordered the invasion of Iraq. The War, as seen by most as illegal and unnecessary, was proclaimed by Bush as a "moral war." We were constantly reminded by Bush that he was proud of all the sons and daughters who had given their lives for their country.

Cyndi, upset over Bush's comment, questioned him as to how he considered this a moral war. Her big question to the president was, "Can you tell me how this war, that my son gave his life for, is considered moral?" She was continually denied access to the president as he embarrassedly avoided her.

There I go getting off the subject again. I keep forgetting that this book is about Racism and not politics. But you know what, in today's political atmosphere, it's all about race! This presidential competition is extraordinarily exciting.

Anyway, let's continue this section of the book entitled "Politics" by injecting a column written in January of 2008 by one of my favorite columnist, Rosa Brooks. Her article, published in the Los Angeles Times, was about the Medias obsession with whether Americans will vote for a Blackman.

In the context of the 2008 election, the question, "Would you vote for a black man for president?" takes for granted certain assumptions: that there is a clearly defined category we can label "black men," that Obama fits into that category and that belonging to that category matters.

Americans over forty may feel justified in their assumption there is a category properly labeled "black men." And of course with his extra melanin Obama fits into that category, right? This makes him black, because "black maleness" matters triggering a set of associations that affect how people think of him.

But increasingly, evidence that younger Americans just don't think about race in the same simplistic ways. Reason being, young Americans are more likely to be minorities themselves. In 2006, only 19.8% of Americans over sixty were minorities compared with about 40% Americans under the age of 40. These young minorities come from a far wider range of racial and ethnic backgrounds than their older counterparts. Once, "minority" largely meant "black," which in turn meant "descendant of Africans brought to the U.S. as slaves.

Today, other descendants like Filipinos, Chinese, Iranians, Mexicans, and Haitians regardless of profession whether it be doctor or construction worker, fit the profile of minority. With the number of inter-marriages going up dramatically over the past few decades so has the number of multiracial young Americans.

Like Obama, these mixtures are neither this nor that, but a bit of this and a bit of that. And unlike older Americans these youngsters are more likely to interracially date, and have close friends of other races.

As a result, race literally isn't a black-and-white issue for many young Americans. Questions like, "Would you vote for a black man?" just don't compute because they assume a reality that's ceasing to exist, in which the term "black" has a fixed meaning, in which Obama's rich heritage can be reduced to a single word.

Rosa Brooks – January 2008

I found this article by Rosa Brooks on racism and the American people, right on target! Some white folks, regardless of education and financial status with a deep history of family racism, would never allow themselves to be convinced to vote for a black man – regardless of their qualifications. This is a sad bit of fact, that today after all the struggles for freedom and equality this country has gone through; there is still a great divide between the races.

I have not been so excited about a presidential race since the one between Nixon and Kennedy. I guess the excitement is enhanced when we have such a strong contrast between candidates.

I remember the political debates in 1960 between Nixon and Kennedy when they were campaigning for the presidency. Obviously color was not a factor in this race, it was all about character! On the nationally televised debates, Nixon came across as gruff, and shifty, while Kennedy was viewed as a classy rich Irish/Catholic.

Although Kennedy won the election as the youngest man ever elected to the United States Presidency, he did not win it by much. Out of the 69 million votes cast, Kennedy won by only 113,000. He got 49.7 percentage of the vote while Nixon got a close 49.6 percentage of the vote - The closest popular vote in 72 years. Kennedy got most of the electoral votes winning the bigger northwestern states – 303 t0 219.

This book was supposed to be finished before the election. I didn't think it would take me this long. I didn't want the election results to influence this section. But, since I've procrastinated so much in this endeavor, the election has come and gone. It was over last week on November 4, and much to my delight, **Obama won!** So I'm gonna extend this article just a little longer to do a little crowing!

Barack Obama, of mixed blood, is a good study of racial confusion in this country. As the son of a white mother from Kansas, and a Black father from Kenya, he had no idea what he was. Born in Hawaii, and Hawaiians being of the same half tone, Barack felt a lot more comfortable with his identity living in the islands.

When he moved to the mainland to begin his education, he discovered a much bigger divide between black and white. Most Americans are still of the mindset that partially black is all black. So Barack, living on the mainland and feeling more at ease with his darker half, decided to go along with his black side. And to further seek acceptance grew an afro and changed his name to Barry.

Recently on Bill Moyers journal on PBS, guest Milissa Harris Lacewell, an African American Professor of Politics and African American Studies at Princeton University admitted: Before Obama first came on the political scene; she didn't consider or know if she wanted a black president. It seemed sort of symbolic. She wasn't particularly attached to the idea of an African American in the white house and like most people of color she thought Barack Obama could not be elected president. She also believed that with a little luck, he might have a chance as Vice President under the wife-cheating white guy, John Edwards.

Professor Lacewell now states, "With Barack Obama winning the election, she was moved to a very profound level about how this made her feel connected to her country in a way she's never fully felt connected before. The notion of Barack Obama being our first bi-racial president is troubling in part – in just about every point of American history, Obama would've been placed in the category of black with all the negatives that go along with it – including beginning with slavery." Professor Lacewell made these statements on Bill Moyers Journal on P.B.S. Jan. 09.

Also a guest on PBS, along with Mrs. Lacewell, was Patricia Williams, author and teacher of law at Columbia University. She too, like Ms. Lacewell is African American and had plenty to say about our new colored president. "Barack, like all blacks, has come to the realization that race is not only biological; it is socially and legally constructed. Barack, with a black father, is considered a bi-racial. African American.

"Part of the innerness in warfare within the black community is based on skin color and the problem with the word bi-racial. How we see our new president centers on our vocabulary of race – First African American or first bi-racial President that could evoke images of a half breed, or a mulatto.

Because of his white mother, people in this country consider Obama more acceptable. With the election of Obama, Blacks for the first time feel truly American – Proud and united with all Americans. An All-Star female basketball player noted: "We no longer feel like distant cousins – At last we have a place at the table"

Bill Moyers closed his show with his own praise of President Barack Obama: "After graduating from Harvard, Barack returned to Chicago where inner city kids with a poor education are more prone to be incarcerated. In his book "Dreams from my father" President Obama wrote, "Upon my return I would find the signs of decay accelerated throughout the Southside - The neighborhood shabbier. The children edgier and less restrained - Middle class families are moving out to the suburbs - Jails bursting with our flowering youth – my brothers without prospects. What have we done to make so many children's hearts so hard, and what collectively can we do to right their moral compass? What values must we live by? Instead, I see us doing what we've always done – pretending that these children are not our own."

Think of Chicago as a metaphor of our country today, where one citizen out of every hundred is in Jail and one out of every ten of those in Jails are black. This is one of the reasons Barack felt he was needed most - and where he could do the most good.

Today is November 6, 2009 and I'm still going through the final process of editing this book. It's taking me a lot longer than I thought. Barack Obama has been president now for over nine months and it's been quite a ride for him. His popularity has taken a hit as it has gone down a bit compared to when he was first elected.

Some of the sore losers and their friends on the other side of the aisle took losing pretty hard. They've taken dirty political tricks to a new high. They now hold Obama responsible for the last eight years. You know, the ones where they were in charge! As the Republicans marched in lock step for Bush, they are just as united in their dislike for Barack Obama. Some, with real hatred, have openly spouted how they hope he fails in his policies! Can you imagine an American citizen of notability openly hoping this country fails?

And because of Barack, and his golden hue, we are also being tested once again as to how racist we are as American citizens. And it doesn't look too good. We've got some real crazies out there who feel as they attend town hall meetings they have to be strapping iron. I just hope Obama, who ran on a platform of change, can in some miraculous way reach some of these nuts.

Part Seven
Business

WHY aren't Minorities as successful as Whites?

First of all, Minorities have no business in business! This country, and all of its worth, was hand-built by people of color who really didn't have much to say about the design and structure of it - Nor did they cash in on its rewards! Minorities were never included in the enacting of laws passed by the government that ruled them - Which also had a big affect on their future and personal lives.

Like our nations founders, most successful stories are about good honest people dedicated to contributing to the greatness of this nation - Unselfish people whose only purpose is improving society in all its aspects. Unfortunately, and as history has proven, successful governments and businesses, once established, attract an element of unsavory unethical types whose main concern is their greed and ambitious agenda.

As kids, we were constantly reminded of how important education was. "Get an education and be a success" was the slogan of the time. But now, as a senior citizen observant of what some of these educated successful aces have done, I kinda question this slogan of old - Maybe it should be, "Get an education and be a success in elevating all societies in health, education, and moral existence."

Success has many meanings to many different people with many different agendas. Unfortunately, most of us in pursuit of success are generally motivated by personal greed. Take guys like Ken Lay and Abramoff who were highly successful in their political and business dealings until they were caught and revealed as white collar criminals. Ken lay died before he could be tried and Abramoff is doing soft time in some club fed somewhere where all white collar criminals go to play. Both Abramoff and Ken Lay (Kenny Boy) were good friends and business associates of President Bush.

In fact! Today Jan. 10, 2009, as I'm writing this section on business, President George "W" had to take time off from planning his own multi-million dollar museum to attend a ceremony where the largest air-craft carrier ever constructed was to be named after his Dad President George H.W. Bush. I wonder how future history books will portray the Bush legacy. Truth or lies.

How's that for getting your just rewards for contributing nothing to a society you promised to serve, honor and protect. The Bush's, along with Vice President Cheney, both in the oil business did all right for themselves under the pretense of serving their country. Some believe the dynamic duo of Bush and Cheney, along with Karl Rove and a few other think a-likes, conned us into the Iraq war because of the oil. I'm not sure about Cheney, but the Bush family, because of their investments in oil, are multi-billionaires!

People are more prone to follow the examples of business and political leaders with the most power and influence. Ambitious young folks prefer to follow the lifestyles of the rich and famous regardless of the questionable methods they used to get there. As today's newspapers confirm, quite a few incompetent successful captains of industry are compensated handsomely for a bad job.

Sadly to say only a minimum amount of good young hopefuls are apt to follow in the footsteps of such greats as Mandela, Gandhi, Chavez, King, and Mother Teresa. This kinda of unrewarding lifestyle, with its sacrifices and unselfishness, isn't too attractive with even the best of us. Thank God for those mentioned above, and hopefully today with Obama in the white house, we'll get that change we need to get back on the moral track.

I personally never had much aspirations or ambition to be someone considered important. As a minority, I've always felt positions of importance were customarily reserved for white folks blessed by God with special abilities and knowledge, deeming me unqualified. As a retired geezer, I now see how naïve and simple I was.

As I grew up, my way of thinking was to lead a simple and uncomplicated life: first by doing some time in the Army, followed by a factory job to support a wife and kids. During that same time in my life, and on the other side of town, white kids were avoiding the draft and going to college. They were smart in getting an education to prepare themselves for that journey to a future of success and riches. Most minorities are generally stuck in dead-end jobs without the option of a career or profession. If only some of us, categorized as Minorities, were brought up thinking that we too can be a doctor, lawyer, or Injun chief!

Anyway, after my stint in the service, I spent 42 years working as a Scenic Artist for the Entertainment industry: Twenty-nine years with NBC, eleven with ABC, and two years as a co-owner of an independent shop. Thirty-three of the forty-two years I worked in top positions as Foreman, Supervisor, and owner. The following is a short bio of my experiences with the white corporate world.

My personal rebellious story against the white man boss

I started in 1958 as a "Paint Boy" in the Scenic Department at NBC Television Studios in Burbank. Although, it was the lowest position in the Scenic Art Department, I was elated with the job that consisted of sweeping and cleaning up after talented artists. At that young age, I would've been content to do it for the rest of my life.

But fate or God had other plans for me. With a bit of talent, luck, and a great love for the job (and to my surprise) in a nine year period I blossomed to where I was a top Scenic Artist. When the position of foreman was up for grabs, three top artists seriously campaigned for the position.

With no real ambition to be the boss, and happy to just paint scenery, I was surprised when the retiring foreman threw my hat in the ring. With a little fear and the insecurities of my ethnicity kicking in, I seriously considered myself an also ran. But as bad luck would have it, I got the job!

The foreman that I replaced (white guy) informed me of how the Supervisor was content to stay in his office and allow the foremen to run things. I was a thirty–two year old boss dealing with a crew of artists who averaged 65 years of age – some out of Vaudeville.

In the next few years my position, along with the department's productivity increased to where I became quite the figure head. The Supervisor had turned it all over to me, including estimating. Because of my ethnicity I worked extra hard to be a success.

It was amusing when new visitors to the department would walk right past my desk in search of the white guy in charge. It was also interesting whenever I interviewed new employees. Minorities either had a meek hat in hand or a large chip on their shoulder. Now white folks, on the other hand, having no discriminatory scars had the natural advantage of their own self confidence and talent.

My problem with the Network began when the Supervisor of the department reached retirement age and his position was available. I was not shocked, and somewhat relieved, that I was not considered for the position. They gave the spot to one of my underlings.

Although I was highly capable of doing the Supervisory job, and again feeling the insecurities of a minority, I accepted the situation gracefully. That is until I heard that management was spreading the word around that I had been offered the position of Supervisor but refused it. Unable to accept this circulating story, I confronted the manager and asked him simply, "Why was he spreading this lie?"

After a lengthy bit of a verbal exchange in his office, and with tight lips, the lying manager reluctantly confessed that he just did not like me! With that said I shook his hand and thanked him for his honesty. In leaving his office, and because of his honesty, I told him that I would not bring the subject up again. This, I believe was the beginning of the end for me at NBC.

Needless to say, NBC put a target on my back and I was subjected to the conventional and unconventional flow of subtle harassment. Most of the abuse was psychological and difficult to prove. I lived with their game playing up to the point of questioning my own attitude and existence. I was beginning to think I was the problem?

That is until the abuse became not so subtle. Like the morning I came to work to find my desk shoved to the middle of the room, completely away from the center of activity. When I tried to shove my desk back to its original and practical spot, the boss stopped me saying, "The manager wanted it moved here!"

On this certain blatant move to discredit me, company managers, department heads and supportive co-workers, circulated a petition stating their disapproval of management's unfair treatment of my desk, my position, and me in general.

Management's response to the petition was to declare my position of Foremen no longer necessary, eliminating my authority completely. From then on, assignments of any significants were doled out to my subordinates as I was assigned menial and demeaning tasks. This drastic change in the department made it kinda awkward as I was now taking orders from my subordinates.

As I reacquainted myself with my paint brushes, and like the days of old, I resurfaced to once again become a top Scenic Artist. So much so, that Art Directors came directly to me for certain jobs. This kinda rubbed management the wrong way. During the many years that I worked as a boss, people had forgotten how good a Scenic Artist I really was - including myself!

I became somewhat of a novelty in the department. Once, while painting a large backing for the "Tonight Show," a group of employees who had only known me as the boss and had never seen me work, gathered around to watch me paint.

Management's plan to break my spirit, by any means possible, backfired as it became apparent my standing in the department was just as strong as ever. It was apparent that my newly found confidence was a disappointment to the higher-ups.

But management being management and after 29 years of my service got in the last lick by firing me. They discharged me on three charges: falsifying a time sheet, an error on a work sheet, and held responsible for a fire of suspicious origin. I was denied my request for the charges in writing. Then when I legally challenged these charges, NBC denied them all together! And to top that off, they denied firing me. They said, "I just left the job!" (My head is still shaking over that one)

Again, a petition by my friends and co-workers was circulated demonstrating their disapproval at my being wrongly terminated. I took my dismissal very hard. I loved my job and the associations that came with it. It was productive and highly enjoyable. Many treasured relationships had been built over the years.

A complaint was filed against NBC - A meeting was called - and a settlement ensued. I'll never forget how ethnic and insignificant I felt as I sat among the battery of NBC attorneys. (All White & Jewish) My representation consisted of an attorney and a Union Representative, also both Jewish. Hey…before you go yelling anti-Semite; let me add that I just wanted to level the playing field with my own two Jews. But to my disappointment against the intimidating battery of NBC attorneys, my representation of two lawyers was weak.

All I got out of my representation was the standard impassioned rhetoric of the unconcerned. I remember when it was over how I sat alone and watched the attorneys (including mine) gathered at the other end of the room giving each other the glad hand.

I was surprised in that the upper echelon of NBC was really not too interested in any of my complaints and charges. They simply wanted the problem to go away. I once asked them if they cared whether I was telling the truth or not. They never answered. But you know what? They must have paid heed to some of my complaints, because soon after my dismissal, the three guys responsible for firing me were forced to resign.

Funny, I didn't get much pleasure out of that. The sad realization of it all was that I was just a dispensable number that had spoke up once too often. All I ever wanted was someone to acknowledge that there was a problem that needed fixing.

I now realize management never would've accepted me as a Supervisor. A close friend of mine (White guy) on the subject of my dismissal honestly revealed his thoughts. He said because of my strong ethnic Latino appearance, I would not look right in a production meeting. I now realize he was right!

During the fifties and sixties, you had to be of a certain type and color to qualify for a position of prominence. In other words, you had to be a white guy. If only I had looked more like Vice Presidents Dick Cheney and Spiro Agnew instead of that union activist Caesar Chavez - I probably would've had more of a chance.

When it comes to abusive behavior and discrimination, I've never had a problem speaking truth to power. One time I was surprised when I hired this black single mom, who really needed work, and she didn't show up for work. She called later that day, and in a teary voice told me she did show up for work but the gate guard wouldn't let her in. The gate guard confirmed her story saying he had been ordered not to let her in. He also added that he thought the manager who put the ban on the black lady, was a little deranged.

I reported the incident to my union representative who filed a complaint which led to the customary fact finding meeting. The meeting, as I was told, was supposed to consist of the Black lady along with the manager responsible for banning her from the lot, his boss, an NBC attorney, our union representative, and myself. But when I escorted the single mom upstairs to the legal department we were met by one lone NBC attorney - A black lady recently hired for this special occasion.

I thought it was typical of NBC's legal dept. to reduce the importance of the situation by not attending the meeting. Obviously, an embarrassed NBC wanted to portray the incident as insignificant and hopefully the problem would go away with a simple apology. This was another racial incident of blatant proportions that they got away with.

To my surprise they not only furnished us with an official apology, but they admitted they had made a serious error. To this day I wonder why big business chooses to go to ridiculous extremes and expense of denial and cover up rather than simply fixing the problem.

I was involved in another issue at NBC involving painting asbestos. The crew of the Scenic Department complained to me about the hazards of painting asbestos without the right protection. I in turn reported their complaint to management. After a bitter battle, the department succeeded in getting the proper equipment.

Although it was a departmental complaint, the same manager who had kicked the black lady off the lot, purposely singled me out as the instigator. I still remember him angrily saying under his breath, "Are you satisfied now?" This manager, whom I had known for years, was a major player in having me fired.

156

This manager is a good example of what is wrong with politics, business, and the corporate world. This type of person brings to mind certain regimes and administrations that continue to exist and operate under such questionable behavior. It's almost like this is the way it's supposed to be!

Anyway, after my experience at NBC I became an independent Artist working out of my garage, house, and yard. Once again I felt my energy and talent return completely free of any emotional and mental distraction. But that didn't last long; I was soon recruited by an independent shop having operational problems. This kept me busy for a year and half as a co-owner until my next venture which involved another major television network.

ABC and Me

My story continues a couple of years later over in Hollywood at the ABC Studios. It was well known through out the Television industry that there was a serious problem in the ABC Scenic Department. Management at ABC was so displeased with the Scenic Supervisor and his assistant that they removed all the authority from the Supervisor and fired the Assistant Supervisor. At that time the department was running rudderless with no one at the helm. This is where I was called in.

With my character and reputation in tack I was asked by ABC if I would apply for the open position of Assistant Supervisor. With the scars still visible from my experience at NBC and a distrust of management or anybody wearing a suit, I without hesitation refused the offer. I was surprised they had asked me since sixteen other hopefuls had applied - Most of them well qualified.

ABC managers were persistent as they continued to woo me until I finally gave in to their offer - But, with a strong condition! I insisted that my position and authority be established and clarified in writing. I did not want a repeat of NBC where my position was very dubious. They agreed and drew up a draft outlining my position. Disagreeing with the wording of the first two drafts, and with a few changes, I finally accepted their third draft.

In my first meeting with management, I told them of how surprised I was at getting the job. I didn't feel I had a chance, thinking they would call NBC for an evaluation of me which would automatically eliminate me. The big boss (Production Manager) said, "On the contrary, he did call his counterpart over at NBC and got a very favorable report of me." He also added that there were a number of people in high places at NBC that thought very highly of me, and concluded they basically felt I was screwed."

After a few months at ABC, NBC's high regard for me was confirmed loud and clear. It happened in the hallway between departments when a group of NBC big shots, visiting the ABC Studios, spotted me and excitedly greeted me with a big warm and friendly hug. Much to my elation, this occurred in front of the ABC Managers.

Before I was hired at ABC, there had been somewhat of a rebellion by the crew in the Scenic Department. This came about because of a steady diet of harassment, and discrimination. The disgruntled crew took their complaints upstairs to voice their objection of the constant abuse of power in the department by the supervisor and his assistant. Because of the strong evidence of this abuse in the Scenic Department, Management had to fire someone, so they fired the boss's friend and foreman.

This is where they brought me in to clean up the mess. They were aware of my reputation at NBC of hiring good talent, and they wanted me to do the same for ABC. They basically wanted me to raise the moral of the crew and the level of quality in the Department. Management suggested I fire one incompetent individual who was kinda running things. I told management I felt like I could deal with situations and personnel without having to fire anyone.

Once in position I hired good competent help to raise the level of talent and productivity in the department – And to the disappointment of management, I didn't fire anyone. Management, on the other hand, was pleased with the results and complimented me regularly on the positive change in the department. Most of the best talent that I acquired came over from NBC. I found out later that these guys that I had hired were referred to by management as "Obie's Boys."

Unfortunately, after a couple of years and to my disfavor, there was a management change - A new white manager from the old school had come to town. This change of personnel had a dramatic negative effect on my position to where it reminded me of NBC. I felt my authority decline as the pattern of leadership took on its old ways of ruling by fear and intimidation.

Unfortunately some of the original rebellious crew, who had complained to management, were once again systematically subjected to mental and emotional abuse. I reported these incidents to management of how the Scenic Supervisor was harassing the crew on a daily basis by verbal harassment with a threat of dismissal. The Scenic crew was more or less blackmailed. I personally encouraged a few of the abused crew members, to report the unwarranted chastising to Management.

Despite telling them I would back them up all the way they responded with bowed heads and slumped shoulders telling me basically the same thing; they refused to report the abuse in fear of getting laid off - or worse, getting fired!

One positive thing I did for the department was to donate scrap paint to a city organization that fought graffiti. Prior to that, scrap paint was hauled away at an expense of $700 a drum. This was a bit ironic since a drum full of good paint cost $500. Management questioned my actions until, through my efforts, they received a letter of appreciation from the city of Los Angeles for their concern about graffiti.

The Supervisor, whose authority had been stripped, was now reinstated and in full command. With his new found power and backing of management, he proceeded to make my life as miserable as possible - So much so that I volunteered for the night crew. But management denied my request, claiming my leadership and scenic expertise would be wasted on the night crew.

NBC and ABC like most major corporations usually circulated memos to all employees to report any infractions of discrimination and abuse of power. The Production Manager at ABC, basically a good leader, had a problem – he was homophobic!

In the entertainment business, gay people because of their creativity are rather prevalent in most departments. And unlike the Army, there is no "Don't ask, don't tell rule."

One morning, before work on my 6:00 AM walk in Griffith Park, I was spotted by the production manager who was out on the golf course doing his morning thing. Later that morning at a staff meeting, the manager mentioned our morning encounter by asking, "What were you doing out there in the park with all those faggots?" I took his question especially hard, not just because I knew at least one of the members in the room was still in the closet, but mainly because my son, also gay, was presently hospitalized with Aides. He had acquired the HIV virus in the late eighties.

My routine, at the time, was spending evenings in the hospital with my son and power walking in the mornings to maintain some stability. In a meeting with "Human Resources" I was asked about abuse of any kind. I reported the "faggot" incident and a meeting with the legal people was called. I was asked of my thoughts on the subject. My opening statement was, "A person of authority, in any kind of a working relationship, should never use a derogatory term in referring to an employee – whether it be Nigger, Spic, Chink, Kike or Faggot."

I also added, this particular manager's discriminatory behavior was practiced on a regular basis. I recounted another meeting in which the Production Manager, an Art Director, and the Supervisor of the Equipment Department were present - And how when the meeting was over, and the Equipment head was barely out of sight, the Manager and the Art Director mimicked the gay Supervisor by giggling and dancing around in a girlish and demeaning manner.

As I stood besides these two people of importance behaving in such a shameful manner, I thought of my son, who had recently passed. I also thought of one of our last conversations where he revealed to me of how it felt being gay. He could not get over how abusively cruel homophobes could be.

When I was asked if I was aware of any other acts or deeds I thought were prejudicial or detrimental to the department, I brought up the foreman of the carpenter shop. A Black man who, although had the most seniority and was highly qualified, was passed over twice for the position of Supervisor - and both times that he was passed over, the position went to a white guy. When he was passed over for the second time it was more than obvious that it was because of his color. Most employees of every color or ethnicity thought highly of this black man and his qualifications.

Everyone figured since he was the foreman of the shop, and next in line for the spot, there was no question that he would get the job. Surprisingly, a few Whites admitted off the record that this was purely a case of racial discrimination. The black man involved was visibly upset and, knowing my history of confronting management and their discriminatory hiring policies, asked me if I would help him.

Before giving him his options of recourse, I reminded him of my personal struggles with the discriminatory ways of management at NBC, and how stressful and lonely the road is when you decide to take them on. One option of his included the E.E.O.C. (Equal Employment Opportunity Commission). One big thing I stressed to him was that once he started on this difficult road he had to stick to it.

He's gotta be prepared to lose a lot of friends - Friends, who will confidentially agree and sympathize with him, but publicly and for their own survival, not say a word. He took my options and personal story home to discuss it with his family.

A week later he told me he had talked it over with his family, and decided not to file a complaint against the company. His reason for not filing was that he was making real good money and did not want to jeopardize his position.

I knew what the black guy was going through. He just wanted the uncomfortable situation to go away. The white guy that got the position was a good friend and co-worker of his. He and the black guy had worked together for years. I'll never forget how embarrassed this white guy was when he revealed to me the only reason he accepted the position was he knew that if he hadn't taken it, someone else would've. I could see his point. The dazzle of a position of importance was too enticing for him.

I was personally saddened by the fact that another case of racial discrimination had occurred. Chalk up another one for the white guys! I remember thinking at the time that if we lived in a perfect world the white manager would've given the job of Supervisor to the deserving black guy, and the white guy who got the job would've never had to compromise himself by taking the job.

My last few years at ABC were not very pleasant. My position was systematically, and on a daily occurrence, reduced to a point where I was deemed ineffective. A good example of my diminished authority was when the ABC News set was moved to a new studio and we had to remove the old paint from the large stage floor. The Supervisor wanted the men to remove the paint using Drano. I told him that Drano was toxic, and I knew hot water and soap would do the job.

He said no, and insisted that the Lye in Drano would be the best thing to remove the paint. As I pleaded with the supervisor about the hazards of using Drano, he ignored me and called the transportation department and had them pick up cases of Drano. Again I stuck my neck out by having a couple of men experiment on a portion of the stage floor by using hot water and soap.

The hot water and soap worked perfectly. When I told the supervisor of how well the soap and hot water peeled the paint right up, he was displeased with my findings. He insisted we stick with Drano. The men again came to me privately saying they refused to use Drano. Already on the outs with management I did not want to stick my neck out any further. I suggested they call the safety department anonymously and report the Supervisor for insisting on the crew using Drano to strip the floor.

After the call was placed, I got a call from an ABC safety guy wanting a confirmation on a phone call he received concerning Drano. It wasn't long after I confirmed the story that a couple of suits showed up knocking on the Supervisors door. We ended up stripping the floor with soap and water and not another word was ever said. However, by the look in the Supervisor's eye, I knew this story was not over. He later proved how much it was not over.

This situation with the Drano reminded me of how I had been whittled down to where I was hesitant in getting involved and speaking up against obvious wrongs. Management, for some reason, continued to back the supervisor one hundred percent no matter what he did.

This brings to mind another incident where the supervisor unfairly chastised a long time employee for something he was not responsible for. Again, I did not speak up! I did however confide in the Artist saying he had a legitimate complaint and if he wanted to go upstairs with it, I would back him up all the way – no matter where it went. But with the usual dejected look and the slumping of the shoulders, he said he could not go through it again. He had challenged the boss once before and was punished with a long lay-off.

The supervisor, along with managements help, did all they could to discredit me and my position. With the exception of the one final incident which I considered to be the last straw, I will spare you the many stories that led me to this point. In February 2000, I along with other department heads attended a production meeting to discuss the Academy Awards. The Art Director, Bob Keene, who I had known for years, and because of our good working relationship directed most of his conversation to me.

Just to prove I'm not an egotistical flake, here's an unsolicited letter of commendation written by the Art Director Robert Keene.

ROBERT
KEENE
+ ASSOCIATES INC
ART DIRECTION

September 28, 1981

Mr. Gino Conte
Director Production Services
NBC TV
3000 West Alameda
Burbank, California 91523

Dear Gino:

I am writing this letter to express on paper how pleased I have been with the Construction Shop, particularly their work on the BOB HOPE SPECIAL #1.

As you may recall, this special was on stage August 27,28,29 & 30th and all of the sets were built in less than a week, one was built overnight, August 26th!

From the beginning there was a tremendous spirit of cooperation between all departments in the construction area and full cooperation and coordination between Construction and Scenic Paint.

It would be impossible to name everyone but I would like to single out a few names.

AL OBREGON: His great attitude helped ease all the tension of a rush job. He also did everything possible to work side by side in direct partnership with the Construction Shop. Even though the hours were very late and very long, all of his men did a fabulous job in the best spirit possible. This is a result, I believe, of his very capable leadership and the respect that each of his men have for him.

CHUCK YEKO: The same thing is true; a great attitude and a real effort to coordinate all departments. Chucks' experience on the floor as a lead man really prepared him for this job. He is a real leader and gets the job done in the best possible way. His lead men, Kjell Bryggman and Lloyd Sletterbak, also assisted in every way possible to make things run smoother.

PAUL NICHOLS: We had a lot of last minute very difficult special effects and he did a great job on all of them.

ED SWIFT: Even though he did not estimate the show, Ed was still involved trying to help coordinate or make suggestions to expedite matters. Ed always goes way beyond the call of duty and trys to be involved and help in any way that he can.

After the meeting, and the fact that the Art Director had singled me out as the one to talk to, the supervisor and managers showed their disdain for me by not allowing me access to the blue prints. Their intentions were obvious in trying to make me look as ineffective as possible - they wanted me sitting stagnant in my office.

Tired of the situation as it was, and knowing what the Art Director wanted, I took the blue prints from the Supervisors office and began to make a few textured samples. When the Supervisor wandered in late as usual and saw what I was doing, he yelled at me for making samples and took the prints away.

He then went upstairs and reported me to the Production Manager for removing the prints from his office. The Manager had his Assistant, and in my presence, tell the Supervisor to assign a singular task to keep me busy. The Assistant Manager and the Supervisor then both agreed that making texture samples for the Art Director would be a good job for me.

I thought this was kinda ironic since making textured samples was what got me into trouble. Realizing I was no longer allowed to function and due to their constant bullshit, I decided to go for broke and bring this ongoing problem to a halt.

I asked the Assistant Manager to set up a meeting between the Production Manager and myself. He obliged and it wasn't long before I was sitting in the manager's office. I opened by telling the manager that in five months I would be sixty-five years of age and able to retire - and since he and I were constantly butting heads, why not give me an early buy-out?

Much to my surprise, I got my buy-out and was out of there in two weeks. Management even gave me a retirement party. During my retirement speech I gave the many attending employees a bit of advice. "Talking back to management can be detrimental to your job." I was given a courtesy laugh by a few.

As an outspoken person at both NBC and ABC I had been labeled a whistle blower and a trouble maker. But whenever I did question management of certain flaws and policies detrimental to the growth of an individual or department, I was very much aware of their discomfort at having a Hispanic approach them on any level.

Over the years as I bitched of the unfairness I had witnessed, the intentions of my objections were always in hopes of correcting a wrong. I never intended to be an advocate of anything, but when pushed with blatant racism I didn't hesitate to voice my objections.

I've always had respect for position - but respect for the individual in position has to be earned! Take for instance the minority with the broom, who while making a minimum wage, does a hell of a job of keeping the place clean. Now this guy, I have a lot of respect for! Then you take the incompetent white-collar boss who is awarded handsomely regardless of how badly he fails in his job.

I also disagree with the business world that has established and maintained separate social classes. This brings to mind a situation I experienced in a network cafeteria. A small group of us were having lunch when an Assistant Art Director (a white lady) joined us at the table. Her boss, an Art Director who I had known and worked with for many years, acknowledged us with a "Hi" as he walked by our table.

This assistant Art Director, who had earned my respect over the years and visa versa, told me later her boss had commented on her sitting at our table. He basically told her she must maintain her higher status as an Art Director and not fraternize with the common folks. Now we could only guess whether the Art Director objected to the fact that we were merely Scenic Artists, or that most of us at the table were of a Hispanic culture. She and I both agreed that this certain Art Director had a problem with minorities.

I have always felt, as human beings, we are all at the same level of existence. What separates us is the circumstance of opportunity. Some of us are much more fortunate than others; like the difference between the rich white kid from the better side of town, and the poor kid from the ghettos or barrios who may have a tougher time finding his niche in life.

I realize one of the reasons for me not falling into step with management is that they tend to insist on complete and unwavering loyalty - And unless you're willing to sacrifice your position and speak truth to power like John Dean did to Nixon, you'll have to swallow your pride and dignity and join the in-group like Bob Halderman and John Ehrlickman.

My dismissal at NBC and my problem at ABC really brought home the point: "You gotta go along if you want to get along."

There are certain levels of the business world reserved solely for whites; usually unapproachable by minorities. Some would argue that there are a lot of minorities in high positions. But in reality those spots, controlled by whites, are usually contractual with a limited time of employment - like in television where you have a lot of minorities doing the news and weather.

These non-permanent jobs that are up for renewal every year or so, are just what the company needs to fill the mandatory quota of minorities ordered by the government. These salaried contract jobs, with a high turn-around rate, are generally controlled by the continual ruling white class.

My experiences, dealing with the major networks, have led me to believe most positions of authority are held and protected by ambitious individuals who will do or say anything to maintain their status. The networks, like in most businesses, are rather rewarding for those at the top – both monetary and position wise. And if their position is threatened or challenged in any way, he or she will immediately pull out all the stops. And if a minority is involved, especially against a white, the white guy will usually prevail.

Jessie Jackson, in 09, on an annual African American meeting stated: In this country, it's a lot easier for a minority to excel in the various sporting arenas than it is to break into the world of business. In sports, the field has been pretty well leveled with athletes of all colors from all over the globe. In fact, one could safely say, minorities are rather predominant in sports. Jessie Jackson's question was, "How come in the business world the playing field hasn't been leveled proportionately to what it is in Sports?"

It's pretty obvious that in sports you're paid and heralded with trophies for publicly performing at a very high level of ability. However, in most businesses as revealed today, all you need to get to the top of the ladder is to be white, ethically challenged, and a practiced ability to bullshit! (Lie)

If it wasn't for manual labor and a periodic war, minorities wouldn't have much to contribute. So let's get on to our next subject where the minorities kinda excel and have a chance to show off – It's about **WAR...**

Which is our next subject!

Part Eight

Minorities in War

Judging from the stories and movies we've heard and seen, minorities have never really played a big part in this nation's defense. It's always about white guys and their unselfish heroics that have saved this nation. So, to set the record straight, I've got a few stories of my own to tell - And being that I'm a Mexican, I'm gonna start right off with Hispanics and their contributions to defending their country.

Starting with my father in the First World War, up to and including the mess George W. Bush got us into in Iraq, there's been about 30 members of my family that have served in defending their country. Two of my brothers, along with two brothers' in-law and some cousins, fought in the big one - WWII. One other brother, and myself, along with other relatives, served during the Korean Conflict - which was considered a police call. Although quite a few of my blood kin were involved in the unpopular war of Vietnam, not too many of them got conned into the war on Terrorism.

This country, in its conflicts, has produced a great deal of heroes. I'd like to take a few lines here and do a little bragging about a cousin of mine, Eugene Obregon. He was a 19 year old East Los Angeles kid born and raised in Pico Rivera. Eugene earned a Medal of Honor posthumously for saving his buddy Bert Johnson's life.

In 1950, during the Korean Conflict, Pfc. Eugene Obregon sacrificed his life for his close friend and fellow Marine, Bert Johnson. While on forward patrol in a little town just outside of Seoul, Bert and Eugene were caught in an ambush by the North Koreans. Bert, who was hit by enemy fire, crumbled in the middle of the street like a rag doll. Nineteen year old Obregon, armed with only a pistol, rushed over to help his buddy who was lying in the street bleeding.

He dragged Bert's bullet riddled body over to a ditch on the side of the road and began to apply bandages. Obregon was soon confronted by a full platoon of advancing enemy forces. Shielding his wounded buddy with his own body he emptied a full clip from his pistol into the oncoming troops. With his pistol empty he grabbed Johnson's carbine and as one man against dozens, continued to fire into the charging enemy. It was only after the carbine was empty, and Obregon had turned to using grenades, that enemy machine gun bullets cut into him killing him instantly.

Obregon's efforts were not in vain, as he had killed twenty-two North Koreans in the process of trying to save his buddy. With time to regroup, the main body of Marines rallied together to rout and defeat the enemy. The next day, and thanks to Pfc. Obregon, the American flag was proudly raised over Seoul. Bert Johnson, a nineteen year old Anglo from Texas, survived his injuries and thanks to his pal Eugene, ended up living a long and happy life.

Surviving eyewitnesses claimed they will never forget the heroism Obregon displayed that September afternoon in saving his buddy's life. Because of the sometimes unbelievable heroics of this story, I felt it necessary to mention the fact that excerpts for this article were taken from two major Los Angeles newspapers - The Los Angeles Times and the Daily News.

On August 30, 1951 Obregon's parents were presented with Eugene's Congressional Medal of Honor. Bert Johnson was present for the ceremony. Unfortunately, stories of Hispanic heroism like Obregons were not considered significant enough for Ken Burns's 15-hour 2007 P.B.S. documentary entitled "The War." After some pressure from the Congressional Hispanic Caucus along with several community and veteran organizations, 28 minutes of footage about Hispanics was added to the documentary.

Private First Class Eugene A. Obregon - USM

Latinos historically, who usually end up with most of the medals, are never really credited for their display of bravery. And when they are credited with going beyond the call of duty and happen to become somewhat of a hero, Hollywood will sometimes honor them with a movie depicting the story of their life. But Hollywood, being Hollywood, will sometimes adjust the ethnicity of the character to make an extra buck.

Here's a good example of Hollywood doing its thing to maintain a certain image of an American hero. During the fifties, Hollywood made a movie honoring Guy Louis Gabaldon, a Latino hero of World War II. This Medal of Honor winner, like Eugene Obregon, was another Mexican kid from East Los Angeles.

I say Mexican kid because most families of that era in Los Angeles were here when it was still a part of Mexico - Thus, generations of Latinos today still considered themselves Mexicans. (Just like native Hawaiians of Hawaii and native Eskimos of Alaska who maintain their original names) My recorded Hispanic family dates back to 1818 when the Southwest was under Spanish rule. Although my mother, who was born in Arizona when it was still a territory, instilled in us kids that we were Americans. She herself referred to all easterners (Gringos) migrating to the southwest, as Americans.

Anyway, back then, there was an area in East L.A. mostly inhabited by Japanese Americans. This is where Guy Gabaldon grew up and having no real home life of his own, he spent most of his growing up time with his Japanese friends and their families.

At age twelve, and mostly on his own, his Japanese friend's family named Nakanos took him in. In living with them, along with learning their culture, he learned to speak the Japanese language fluently. He lived with the Nakano family up **until...**

The Japanese attacked Pearle Harbor on December 7, 1941

President Roosevelt, calling it a day of infamy, immediately declared war on Japan. All American citizens of Japanese ancestry, and because of a strong fear of sabotage, racial prejudice, and economic rivalry, were looked upon as a threat to the nation's security.

Because of this so-called threat, American civil liberties were cast aside as Japanese American citizens, living in California, were uprooted forcing them to sell all of their properties.

Imagine who took advantage of this sweet deal

"Guy Gabaldon was upset when the U.S. Government put Japanese-Americans in Concentration Camps, which included his adopted parents. (A quote by Guy Gabaldon's wife Ohana)

Courtesy of California State Library

Japanese Americans Forced to sell their homes in exchange for a barbed wire enclosure. (This was happening about the same time the Jews in Germany were being rounded up for their own special fate)

Eighteen year old Guy Gabaldon, finding himself alone and separated from his Japanese family, enlisted in the Marines. Ironically, he was shipped to the Pacific Islands to fight the Japs. Yeah, he was trained to kill the same kind of people that raised him! At first he had a problem with the fact that his friends, the Japanese people, were the enemy. He liked them! He spoke their language!

So, rather than fight and kill the Japanese with weapons, he used his knowledge of the Japanese language to convince the enemy to surrender. He'd go out at night by himself roaming Saipan's caves and pillboxes, persuading enemy soldiers and civilians to surrender. He told them in their language that the Marines would not torture them as advertised, but would feed them and give them medical care.

He warned them of their sure death if they stayed hidden in their caves. Eighteen year old Guy was pretty convincing as he coaxed the enemy to lay down their weapons and follow him back to the American side. He once captured a Company of Japanese all by himself. By the end of the battle of Saipan, Gabaldon singularly had captured over 1,000 Japanese by convincing them to surrender.

Guy's heroic story was so impressive; Hollywood was interested in making a movie of his life.

Guy Louis Gabaldon – Mexican American War Hero
(I guess Guy could pass for an Italian, but it would take
a lot of squinting to pass him off as Jeffrey Hunter)

But Hollywood, being Hollywood, had to make a few changes. Their big problem was that Guy Gabaldon was a little too ethnic. (Mexican) So, to give the story more credibility they felt they had to cast an actor that best represented America - You know the usual fair-haired blue eyed white guy type.

Hollywood immediately thought of Jeffery Hunter to play the part of the heroic Gabaldon. Yeah, the same guy that played Jesus Christ in the movie "King of Kings!" And to further stretch the truth, they changed Guy Gabaldon's ethnicity from Mexican to Italian. There! That should sell a lot more tickets!

In Los Angeles, Latinos, who by numbers disproportionately serve in the armed services; have received more than there share of medals of valor. In 1943, During the Second World War, and despite the number of Latinos serving their country, there was an all time high of racism against Hispanics on the home front.

Young Latinos, who were not serving, were not content to stay within the confines of their Barrios. They wanted to get out and enjoy some of that night life that was going on. So they left the security of their barrios and spilled out into the streets of downtown Los Angeles where they frequented night clubs, dance halls, and movies houses.

To further distinguish themselves as individuals, these young men created their own style of dress that became known as the "Zoot Suit" look - An ensemble that consisted of broad shouldered long coats, wide brimmed hats, and high-waisted peg-legged trousers with a long chain. They were known as "Pachucos."

Because of the war, Los Angeles's population grew with military personnel newly stationed here from other parts of the country. Most of these white guys had never seen a Mexican before, or read a book about how the Southwest was once owned by Mexico. So when Los Angeles Newspapers tagged the young Mexicans as trouble makers, the white military guys took the bait.

These new newcomers to the city, fired up with patriotism and bigotry, jumped right on the hate wagon and took their liberty pass to town. It all began when a few sailors claimed they had been beaten and robbed by Mexican Pachucos. In retaliation to the beating, 200 sailors hired a fleet of cabs and rolled into East Los Angeles to beat up and strip any young male Latinos they could find.

Emboldened by the lack of response by the LA authorities, and for several subsequent nights, mobs of sailors and soldiers along with some civilians, invaded the Mexican barrios of the east side.

They marched together side by side down the streets invading bars and movie houses assaulting and humiliating any and all young Latinos whether they were wearing Zoot Suits or not. As Mexican bashing became a popular and accepted sport, and due to a backlash from the Mexican community, police were ordered to keep an eye on the caravans of rioting servicemen. Police were told to just observe and let the shore patrol and military police handle it.

Because of the magnitude of the riots, police finally intervened as they tried to stop the mess they had allowed to fester. Police arrested and charged over 500 Latino youths for vagrancy and rioting – many of them victimized by the servicemen as 150 of them were injured. Once again the white guys win.

The local press lauded the military rioters for confronting the menace of the "Mexican Crime Wave." The Los Angeles Times proudly displayed this headline, "Zoot Suiters Learn Lesson in fight with Servicemen." The City council went so far as to issue an ordinance banning the wearing of Zoot Suits. Even Blacks and Filipinos, were accosted for simply being minorities. This all took place within a week's time. Finally on June 7, military heads tired of the lack of the city's authority in dealing with the riots took matters into their own hands – they declared Los Angeles off-limits to all military personnel.

The slow and inadequate response by L.A. authorities in dealing with the rioting military personnel drew national condemnation. President Roosevelt's wife, Eleanor Roosevelt showed her displeasure with the City of Los Angeles by a publicized comment,

"The question goes deeper than just Zoot Suits. It is a racial protest. I have been worried for a long time about the Mexican racial situation. It is a problem with roots going a long way back, and we do not always face these problems as we should."

The Los Angeles Times on June 18 responded to the first ladies comments with headlines reading, "Mrs. Roosevelt blindly stirs race discord." Editorial pages accused her of communistic ways.

Although the County Board of Supervisors appointed committees, and launched an investigation into the riots, the only victims of any real consequence were the Latinos arrested during the riots. Mayor Fletcher Bowen, in response to local opinion and the Mexican Embassy, tried to downplay the racial character of the situation, by blaming Mexican youth gangs for inciting the riots. To improve race relationships with Hispanics, the Police Department was instructed to train its officers in treating all citizens of all colors equally. Yeah, that should do it!

But all in all, as far as discrimination in the armed forces is concerned, Mexican Americans had it pretty easy compared to African Americans and Japanese Americans.

We're all aware of how badly and unjustly the Japanese Americans were treated after the attack on Pearl Harbor, but the only reason our darker hued African Americans were treated badly was because they were… eh…African Americans.

Due to a well orchestrated propaganda machine, real Americans were taught to hate all Japanese people – Japanese American citizens as well! I thought it odd as we singled out only the Japanese people when we were also at war with Germany and Italy - yet we were not taught to hate them! That is with the exception of a few Germans proven to be spies, not too many Italians or Germans were locked up.

Obviously, because of their European ancestry they were considered too American to lock up. I hope we never go to war with Mexico! Despite all this hatred and bigotry against the Japanese, there was a group of interned Japanese American men who volunteered to fight for their country. They were released from internment camps, and trained in special warfare. These proud Americans were assigned to fight in Africa and Germany.

These Japanese Americans, because of their outstanding work in the fields of battle against the Germans, ended up being decorated heroes. One of those brave heroes was a guy by the name of Daniel Inouye of Hawaii. Dan, who is now a Senator, was physically disabled while serving his country in WWII.

Daniel Inouye was a young resident of Pearl Harbor when it was bombed by the Japanese on that day of infamy, December 7, 1941. With confusion and chaos running amok, Danny Inouye, a seventeen year old Red Cross volunteer, jumped in to help wherever he could. He was assigned to handle the bodies of the dead and wounded that lay scattered about.

One vivid memory Inouye had of that day is when he ran over to help a mother holding her crying baby, he immediately went into shock as he discovered the mother's head had been blown off. This, he says is a vision he will never be able to shake.

Even with all the heroics, Inouye and the other brave Japanese men were still scorned and looked upon as the enemy. Adding insult to injury, during the Nixon Watergate Senate Investigation, Senator Dan Inouye was referred to on a live microphone as a, "Damn Jap." And this was from one of his esteemed fellow Senators!

After the war, and with everything getting back to normal, we freed the Japanese people from the camps. They were allowed to return and make do with what they no longer owned or had. My dentist, a Japanese American, who was interned at the age of two years old, remembers vividly the day he was freed. As a five year old kid his first big excitement was seeing a city for the first time. He could not get over the sight of the brightness of the lights and neon signs that lit the city – he thought it was magic! Another Japanese American acquaintance of mine was born at Manzanar internment camp in the High Sierras of California.

Blacks in War

Blacks, or Negros as they were called in those days, were considered by many as lacking in intelligence, skill, courage, and patriotism. Back then, they were never really considered to be a full human being. These black soldiers were recruited and trained to serve in the motor pool as drivers and mechanics.

However, there was a select group of young black men who enlisted in the Air Force and became famously known as the Tuskegee Airmen. These dedicated and determined young men possessed the physical and mental qualifications to be accepted as aviation cadets. They were trained specifically as single-engine or double-engine pilots, navigators or bombardiers.

They came from all parts of the country, with the larger numbers coming from big cities like New York, LA, and Chicago. Each enlistee possessed a personal desire to fight for their country. They were trained at Tuskegee Army Air Field in Tuskegee, Alabama.

The first black aviation cadet class began training in July 1941 and finished nine months later in March 1942. Out of the thirteen that started the class, five received their silver pilot wings. From 1941 to 1946, nine hundred and ninety-four Negros received their wings as they graduated from Tuskegee as commissioned pilots.

Tuskegee Army Air Field Airmen

Other blacks, in selected military bases scattered about the country, were trained to be navigators, bombardiers, and gunnery crews. Four hundred and fifty pilots trained at Tuskegee, served overseas in either the 99th Fighter Squadron or the 332nd Fighter Group. They flew P-40 Warhawks in combat in North Africa, Sicily, and Italy.

Besides fighting the war in Europe, Black service men had to fight racism here at home. Many of the black airmen, who did not go overseas, were trained at Selfridges Field, Michigan as bomber crews.   These highly trained Black men, regardless of the fact they were officers in the Army Air force, were treated as lowly trainees. They were denied access to the officer's club - An act contradictory to Army regulations.

These black officers, knowing their rights as US Airman, questioned heatedly as to why they were denied access to the club. The Army, felt the best way to stop the trouble was to ship these black trouble makers to Godman Field, Kentucky.

The trouble did not stop at Godman field, as the unfair treatment and hostility against the black officers continued. So once again the black trouble makers were shipped out - This time to Freeman Field, Indiana where they were ordered not to try to enter the officers club.

The situation of racism practiced by the white guys was just as intense at Freeman Field as was experienced at other fields. Open hostility toward the blacks finally climaxed when black officers, and against direct orders, tried to enter the Freeman Field Officers Club.

For their act of defiance in demanding their equal rights as American officers, a melee broke out resulting in the arrest of one hundred and three black officers. They were charged with insubordination and ordered to face a court martial.

Court martial proceedings were quickly dropped against one hundred of the officers. Of the remaining three, two of them eventually had their charges dropped. But it took fifty-years to finally convict the third officer, Lt. Roger Terry. Officer Terry's court martial conviction was then reversed and his military record cleared. As of this date, all one hundred and three officers have had their military records purged of any reference to the Freeman Field incident.

After the war ended in 1945, returning black men continued to face open racism on military Forts and bases in the good old USA. In 1948, because of this ongoing racism, President Harry Truman enacted Executive Order Number 9981 directing equality of treatment and opportunity for all men in the U.S. Armed Forces.

This order led to the end of racial segregation in the military forces - and a big step in leading to the beginning of segregation in America- the land of the free. Finally, our warriors of all colors were to be appreciated and treated as equals.

SPEAKING OF WARRIORS

To a Native American, the warrior tradition is an old one. A warrior is characterized with strength, courage, wisdom, and honor and possesses a willingness to engage the enemy in battle.

The Native Indians didn't become American citizens until the Indian Citizenship act of 1924. This was granted primarily by the fact that over 12,000 Native Americans had served in World War One.

Native Americans, because of their new status as US Citizens, became eligible for the draft. So when World War 2 broke out, these new redskin citizens were summoned right along with the toe heads from Nebraska.

More than 40,000 of these Indian braves fought the Germans and the Japanese in World War Two. Then in Viet Nam, over 42,000 returned to the battlefield to again fight for Uncle Sam.

Because of the broad call of the draft for Americans from border to border and coast to coast, the merging of all ethnicities were brought together to fight a common foe. This is where Native American Indians had to leave the comfort (?) of their reservations and forced to live and breathe with the rest of America.

This forced young racists of any color to deal with other ethnicities in the confines of their barracks on a daily basis.

As an Army veteran of the early fifties, I recall men of all levels of society having to eat, sleep, and live together as one. It was also interesting to see the combination of colors, cultures, and social levels pair off in friendships - Combinations, which in this country, to the average Middle American would normally appear as odd.

You throw a mixture of colors, cultures, and personalities together in a barrack, and in time you will soon see a well adjusted, non-racist group of men and women standing tall, side by side.

Because of the uniqueness of the Navajo language, a special group of Navajos became famously known on the Pacific front as Code Talkers. These code talkers were used in communications to prevent the Japanese from deciphering any of their messages.

Navajo Code Talkers

Another Native American that made the hero list is a woman by the name of Lori Piestewa who was raised on a Navaho Reservation in Arizona by her Mexican mother and Hopi father. She was the first American Native woman to die in battle on foreign land.

Lori's home land was not always an Indian reservation. It once was farming land for the Hopis. But the white government, during the late 80's, had the US Calvary take the lands away from the Hopi's and give it to the invading white settlers.

The Hopis didn't take to well about loosing their land. In defiance of the white mans decree, they put their bows and arrows aside and continued to illegally cultivate their lands. When the army got wind of these peaceful people plowing the same fields their fathers had plowed, they were arrested and imprisoned in Alcatraz - some were put in solitary confinement for up to two years.

The word Hopi means "Peaceful People." Lori's Father, Terry Piestewa, - who fought in Vietnam, believed they were put on this earth to be peaceful. Terry, who was influenced by the fact that his two older brothers were imprisoned for refusing to fight in the Korean Conflict, had no choice but to go along with Uncle Sam's wishes. Terry, a peaceful man, is not too proud of what he did in Vietnam.

But that was then, and this is now. Lori Peistewa, unlike her father and uncles, was proud to sign up to defend her country against a horrific enemy - An enemy that President Bush said had weapons of mass destruction and was not afraid to use them.

The Bush Administration's propaganda really had us in fear of a nuclear attack by these "Weapons of mass destruction." All that would be left is a big cloud of smoke. Bush also reminded us regularly that our grandchildren would be annihilated too!

Anyway back to Lori Piestewa who was assigned as a driver with the 507th Army Maintenance Company in Iraq. On March 23, 2003 (three days into the war) she and seventeen other trucks loaded up with clerks, cooks, and repairman were a support group for the main convoy of 600 vehicles. But somewhere along the line Lori's team of 28 trucks fell behind the main group causing them to get lost.

Lost and confused, they took a wrong turn and ended up in a little town called Nasiriyah. Without warning, Lori's company suddenly found themselves surrounded and fired upon by Iraqi soldiers. The Iraqis blasted the lost convoy with AK-47s, mortars, and rocket-propelled grenades. This is where Lori Piestewa, along with ten other soldiers, was killed.

There were also nine other soldiers wounded in the attack described as a "torrent of fire." One of the nine wounded was Lori's best friend and roommate Jessica Lynch. Though very few of us recall Lori Piestewa's story, we are all aware of the saga of Jessica Lynch who was wounded and captured in that fiery ambush. Because of Jessica's severe wounds the enemy placed her in an Iraqi hospital. Days later, she was rescued by American soldiers and rushed to safety. The heroic scene was taped to prove the authenticity of the rescue – Also wounded severely on that day was the **TRUTH.**

Combat Buddies – Jessica Lynch & Lori Piestewa

This picture was taken at Fort Bliss Texas, the day before they were deployed to Iraq)

At that time in our history, the Bush Administration was still trying to sell the un-preempted invasion of Iraq. They even gave the "War in Iraq" a new title, Bush and Cheney labeled it "Operation Iraqi Freedom." So hoping to capitalize on Jessica Lynch's story and promote Bush's agenda, it was decided to forego the truth and crank up the story a bit.

As it was first revealed, and besides her initial wounds, Jessica was reported to have been shot. It was also reported that the medical staff abused the wounded by slapping them around - AND, to really enhance the story, we were told Jessica had been brutally raped.

Why do they always have to play the rape card - Especially when it involves a young blond girl and a guy with dark skin? Does being blond give it more of a punch? Well, the gullible media was quick to oblige as they were taken in by the shrewdness of the Bush Administration's propaganda. Jessica Lynch's story was presented to the American public as a real-life type Rambo – **a "GI- Jane."**

Early press reports read, "Jessica did not want to be taken alive as she emptied her M-16 while being fiercely stabbed and shot multiple times – An unnamed military official described Jessica as a "Blond warlike female boldly fighting to the end."

U.S. citizens were joyful in the fact that we had a real live war hero in the shape of a pretty blond girl from Middle America. When the Government was through applauding Jessica for her bravery, she was welcomed in her home town with all the pomp of a hero.

But sadly for the Bush Administration, and the US Army war promoters, the truth rose to the surface, and "surprise, surprise," it was all a big lie! The American people were once again lied to by the US Government. What is it with some people in power who honestly...NO, STRIKE THAT, I mean "dishonestly" feel because of their position they can lie to promote their agenda.

Jessica was disappointed when she first heard of how she was being falsely portrayed as a war hero. "I am not a Rambo type GI Jane" she spouted every chance she got in denying the ridiculous spin they were putting on her story. She also realized the Government needed a war hero to further promote the recruitment of the war - but must they be such big liars in doing so?

When asked who she thought were the real heroes, and without hesitation Jessica would say, her best friend Lori Piestewa, who was killed trying to get her and the others to safety as they were being ambushed. She also praised the rest of the soldiers that died during the ambush – and of course, the men that rescued her. "These are all the real heroes." One of her best quotes on heroism was, "The real heroes are those who speak and insist on the truth, and not the ones that falsely hype a story for their own agenda."

With the government's face still red from all the lies they made up to promote Jessica Lynch's capture in Iraq on March 23, 2003, they did it all over again one year later on March 22, 2004 when Pat Tillman, a native of San Jose Californian, was shot and killed. Because of the terrorist attack on 911 Pat Tillman, a true patriot gave up a lucrative career with the Arizona Cardinals, (NFL) to volunteer and help win President Bush's war in Iraq.

Pat was accidentally killed in Iraq by friendly fire. (American troops) This is where the Government saw another opportunity to open up a new chapter on the making of a government hero. Pat Tillman was the perfect guy to promote as a hero. He was a tough ex-football player with ranger training - a real Rambo type guy in any sense of the word.

The first thing the government did was stifle the truth and report that Pat Tillman had been killed by enemy fire. The government put a gag order on anyone and everyone that knew what really happened. The last soldier to see the NFL hero alive was silenced by authorities. He later testified that he was ordered not to divulge the truth – to anyone!

Pat Tillman's folk, because of the governments altered and fuzzy accounts of what happened to their son, would not accept the results of the government's investigations. So with pressure from all involved to find the truth, a committee was formed to find out what the hell really happened to Tillman!

What is it with these guys in power, they're like little kids who think all they have to do is lie and the problem will go away. And when caught, they follow that up with another lie. Do they really believe in the Nixon theory that if those in power say it, it's gotta be true!

This House Committee on Oversight and Government Reform, headed by Senator Henry Waxman (D-Ca) was created to investigate the misleading military statements following the death of Tillman. Secretary of State, Donald Rumsfeld, when called to testify and under oath said, "There was no evidence of a cover up of the circumstances of Tillman's death,"

When Jessica Lynch heard what Rumsfeld had to say, and knowing how the government could spin a story, stepped up to the mike and gladly testified in behalf of the Tillman family. Lynch accused the Government of fabricating the story as part of the Pentagon's propaganda to promote the war.

Jessica's real heroism was realized when instead of going along with the government and their lies, stood tall and spoke truth to power just for the sake of doing what was right. Not too many of us would give up all the medals and parades that go with being a war hero to testify against the government in a truth finding investigation.

The outcome of the investigation never really revealed who was guilty. Before the truth came out about Tillman, the Republicans considered him "The right wing poster child for the war" - That is until they heard Tillman had regarded the invasion of Iraq as illegal.

Let's get back to Jessica's friend Lori Piestewa, who Jessica says is the real hero. How come she didn't get no big ol' splash of government and media press on her story. If it wasn't for Jessica bringing out the real story of Lori to the American people, we never would've heard of her. Is our government that simple, or do they naturally assume we are all that simple.

Pat Tillman & Jessica Lynch – Real American heroes

Another good friend of Jessica involved in that mess in Nasiriyah was a black female soldier by the name of Soshanna Johnson. She never got much of the limelight either. It's kinda surprising that Jessica Lynch, a pretty white blond from Middle America, would pick as her best friends two women, one Black and one Indian. Oh, and to top it off she got engaged to a Mexican guy - Sergeant Ruben Contreras. For reasons much too obvious, he didn't get much press either.

The white social class in power, and for their own agenda, continue to push an image they think best portrays the real America. They prefer the image to be a White person resembling Timothy McVeigh or Dick Cheney. Eh…No wait, come to think of it Mr. Cheney, because of multiple deferments, didn't have to serve. – McVeigh however, was awarded citations of valor for fighting in the Gulf War.

Let's take a look at the next subject which is entertainment and see if that's any different.

Part Nine

ENTERTAINMENT
Racism in the Movies & TV

Colored People, Blacks & African Americans

Remember the good old days when the roles in the movies of Maids, Butlers, and Chauffeurs were played by Black People - People like Stepin Fetchet, Haddie McDaniel, and Rochester? In those days Negros were upgraded to the level and title of "Colored People.

Blacks, Negros, Colored People or African Americans were usually used in the movies in menial or servitude roles - Especially if they needed someone good with a mop who could shuffle along as they answered to the white man with a smiling, "Yah-suh Boss!" – All this while singing a woeful song.

And if Hollywood needed someone to play a smart and presentable Negro, they'd take a white girl and black her up. Leila Bennett, a white girl, played the role of a maid in black face. - In those days it wasn't considered insulting to the colored folks.

Leila Bennett and Janet Gaynor in "The First Year"

More about "Whities" in blackface: Al Jolson (1886 - 1950) American stage and film performer was born Asa Yoelson in Seredzius, Russia. Jolson is most noted for performing as a minstrel-style singer in blackface – which became his vaudevillian trademark. Al Jolson starred in the 1927 motion picture "The Jazz Singer," a movie credited with being the first important picture with sound.

I found the information in researching Al Jolson typical of most sources of information. Although Asa Yoelson was born in Russia, with a strong foreign sounding name, Encarta chose to recognize and introduce him as an "American stage and film performer." Yet anyone else in this country, not of European ancestry, and regardless of how long they've been a citizen of the USA, is usually referred to by their ethnicity. Examples: Denzel Washington is an African American film star – Edward James Olmos is a Mexican American stage and film performer. Hmm…I wonder why that is?

Then there's "Amos and Andy," one of the biggest, if not the biggest, comedy teams of all time. The creators and original portrayers of the radio show "Amos and Andy" were two white guys, Freeman Gosden and Charles Correll. They performed in blackface as they played the roles of two African Americans. It was one of the most popular highly rated radio shows in history.

The series premiered in 1928 on NBC radio. The impact of the show was a phenomenon. Because of the unpredicted popularity and success of the show it is said cities literally came to a halt while the show was on the air. Everyone loved these two guys and their daily antics. While the peak of their popularity happened during the thirties, the show remained on the air for a total of thirty years. The show moved to television in 1951 where it ran until 1953.

We also had movies made specifically for Colored people.

There was a movie starring Bill Pickett called "The Bull-Dogger" "World's Colored Champion." This movie was made with an all black cast primarily for a black audience. The poster came with an optional placard reading, "See it at your favorite colored theater."

Most of us had never heard of Bill Pickett the world famous cowboy who performed for such notables as Teddy Roosevelt and the King and Queen of England. His specialty, which he invented, was leaping off a horse onto a racing steer which he would force to the ground. Pickett, a fabulous character who was breaking horses at age seventy, rode with such greats as Tom Mix and Will Rogers. He is comparably revered today with William S. Hart. One member of the cast, Bennie Turpin, was the Black version of Ben Turpin, the popular cross-eyed comic of the twenties and thirties.

Another movie with an all colored cast was "The Fight Never Ends" starring the heavy weight champion of the world, Joe Lewis "The Brown Bomber." I'm sure this movie with an all black cast starring Ruby Dee, The Mills Brothers, Harrel Tillman, Emmett (Babe) Wallace, and Gwendolyn Tynes, invited whites to cross the racial color line at the theaters.

As of this date, December 2008, Blacks have been integrated and elevated in the movies to where they now play roles of distinction and importance - Like Judges, lawyers, and Police Chiefs. No more shuffling around as janitors or wailing prisoners. And if their real good looking and can sound white, they may get a shot at a major role as a white guy's side kick.

This brings to mind a young Bill Cosby who played opposite Robert Culp in the popular TV series "I Spy." Because of the shows success, Cosby went on to bigger and better things. He eventually got his own show "The Bill Cosby Show" where he played an upper class doctor named Huxtable, with a wife and three kids. The Cosby sit-com was about an average American Family, with average problems. The show was a huge success and I believe its popularity was due to the fact that it was not about a black family, but an American family. Bill Cosby's family color was never a concern of the show.

Today's highly successful black entertainers like Eddie Murphy, and Will Smith, are paid multi-million dollar salaries for a movie – and they get to pick their own roles too! Then there's Halle Berry who gets whatever she wants, whenever she wants it. Yeah!!

Richard Pryor was another black entertainer that hit the big time. I remember, while doing a comedy special at NBC Television Studios in Burbank, Richard insisted on an all black production staff. NBC's big-wigs agreed and were able to fill the bill with only one exception - They couldn't find a Black Art Director.

After an exhaustive search of Hollywood, and the Los Angeles area, not one black Television Art Director could be found. This proved to be embarrassing for not only NBC and the Art Directors Guild, but for the entire entertainment industry.

The government's general embarrassment of the racial imbalance in the entertainment business set up a program to correct the problem - or give the appearance of trying. This program was originally implemented to help minorities integrate into the lucrative world of Hollywood. The networks created a mixed working force by hiring minorities to work side by side with whites, in hopes minorities would learn something from the smarter and more talented whites.

Minorities were hired at TV and Motion Picture studios in the various production departments where they worked on a trial basis at six month intervals. They then were rotated between departments to learn other aspects of the business. This federally funded program, like most federally funded programs looked good on paper, but when put into motion, fell right on its face.

I witnessed one situation where a boss of a department allowed a young minority to spend the entire day talking to his girl on the phone. When I questioned the boss about the talkative and idle minority, he shrugged his shoulders saying, "Why should I concern myself...the whole thing is a big joke!"

The problem with the program was that young minorities, being young minorities, did what young minorities usually do without adult supervision - They did what ever they damn well pleased!

However, in most creative departments employees were hired more on artistic talent than on their heritage or color. These departments had no problem filling their quota of minorities. Take the Scenic Department for instance; because of its variety of race and culture, it was called the League of Nations. Creative departments had to rely mostly on artistic ability, as opposed to being white with a gift of gab.

But for obvious reasons, the real good paying jobs with positions of authority were pretty well taken up by white guys who did everything imaginable and unimaginable to keep those high paying jobs. Believe me, as mentioned in the Business chapter (7), I know from personal experience the ways and means of certain insecure management personnel who will go to great lengths in protecting their territory.

Out of the 42 years in the business, thirty-three in position of authority, my happiest time was just painting scenery as a regular Scenic Artist. When I was first promoted to Forman, and six months into the job, one of the older Artists reminded me of how much I had changed. He said he used to love to hear me sing and whistle on the job – something I didn't do anymore.

The position of authority was a level of authority I had never considered or really wanted. Growing up in this country, I was pretty well programmed to believe positions of prominence and authority were reserved for guys that looked more like Dick Cheney and Spiro Agnew, than Martin Luther King Jr. and Caesar Chavez.

My confrontations with management and their policies eventual led to my dismissal which began my trek down that bumpy and lonely road to "Disgruntle Ville."

Most racism practiced on individuals in the corporate world is psychologically subtle where no visible scars can be found. And those in authority, with the help of their legal goons, can usually explain and justify all charges of racism as nonsense. Hmmm...

However, sometimes racism is so blatant; it cannot be explained by any legal eagle. One embarrassingly good example happened at NBC during the sixties. It was during the taping of a commercial for a Chevrolet automobile. The script called for a couple (man and a woman) to enter from stage left and stroll over to a new Chevrolet car sitting on center stage - The man and woman were entertainers; Harry Belafonte, and Petula Clark – a black man and a white woman.

Harry and Petula entered from stage left as scripted. They sauntered over to the Chevrolet causally holding hands. The director up in his booth yelled, "Stop...Stop taping, I'll be right down." Everything, and everyone, shut down as they waited for the director to come down from his white tower.

Once on stage, the director walked over to Petula and Harry and questioned the hand holding. He loudly and clearly complained, "America is not ready to see a White woman holding hands with a Black man."

All the people on stage stopped what they were doing and nervously stared at the Director. This little incident created quite an uproar resulting in the director's eventual dismissal. I happened to witness this blatant bit of racism live and in color.

Orientals in Entertainment

People from the Orient and all points east, are no longer called Orientals, they are now called Asians. Growing up in the forties, as a Mexican kid in East Los Angeles, my memory of Asian people is very limited. - I can only recall a vegetable market owned and operated by a Chinese family.

And in the early movies, Chinese people usually played parts calling for a sweaty cleaner guy, or a gardener. That is with the exception of the world famous detective, "Charlie Chan." Charlie was a real cool sleuth who could out-detective Sam Spade and Phillip Marlow. Someone once told me that the guy that played Charley Chan was not really Chinese - he was a White guy! I didn't believe it at first; I knew he had to be Chinese because he had a Chinese son! Anyway, it was later proven to me that the guy who played Charlie Chan was actually a Swedish guy by the name of Warner Oland.

Warner Oland first played Charlie Chan in 1926 in a serial filmed at Twentieth Century Fox. In those days serials were popular among both kids and adults. The serial was such a success; the studio followed it up by making nearly fifty movies of the Asian sleuth.

But for some reason, after a few movies, Warren Oland was replaced as Charlie Chan by another actor. And Yup, It was another white guy by the name of Sidney Toler.

Most, if not all, of Charlie's movies were made in black and white and considered to be "B" movies. If Mr. Chan was still in business today, and with his special detective techniques, he'd be right up there with Colombo and Monk.

Nowadays, Chinese people along with everyone else have more than Charlie to root for - We've got those bad-ass marshal arts guys' Bruce Lee and Jackie Chan. These two Chinese stars, known world wide as experts at Karate and Judo, have made a fortune beating up bad guys. Their loyal fans consist of all brands of people, regardless of color.

A far as Chinese woman are concerned, I can only think of a few ladies that made it big. One was Nancy Kwan who was half white. She starred in the movie "The World of Susie Wong" co-starring William Holden who played the male lead in this blockbuster movie.

Another biggie of that era, and considered to be one of the great love stories of all time, was the movie "Love is a Many Splendored Thing." This movie was about an American guy and a Chinese nurse. The nurse was played by Jennifer Jones and her love interest was none other than super-star William Holden - Yeah, he had a thing for Chinese gals. Hey, wait a minute, Jennifer wasn't Chinese! But so what, she did a good job of playing one.

Come to think of it, there were a few other white folks that played Asians. Peter Lorre as the "Amazing Mr. Motto" - Lee J. Cobb in "Attila the Hun" - and remember John Wayne as the "Barbarian?"

"Then we have the dirty sneaky Japs"

Because of the sneak attack on Pearl Harbor December 6, 1941 we Americans were effectively programmed via propaganda posters and the Saturday matinee to hate all Japanese people. As a youngster in the 40's, I was programmed to believe that Japanese people were sneaky little yellow people who wore glasses and had big buck teeth.

It was common to see audiences at the movies boo and hiss the Japs as they chased John Wayne and other super stars around the war torn skies in their flying Zeros. Their planes, which always outnumbered the Duke, equipped with machine guns would fire in vain at the Duke in hopes of bringing him down.

But eventually, and as the script dictated, Big John would soon turn the tables around on those dirty yellow "Nips" and the boos would turn to cheers as John Wayne blasted the Japanese zeros out of the sky sending them spiraling downward in a cloud of smoke.

See, what I mean!

But you know what? If it wasn't for all those war movies starring John Wayne and the likes, Japanese people would've never been cast in any movies at all. A few familiar faces of Japanese actors were seen in most war movies, even if it was just portraying the same ol' bad guy.

Mexicans in the Movies

(This includes Hispanics, Latinos, Spics, wetbacks and all other Brown People that fit the category)

Mexicans have been involved in the movies since the days of the silent movies. But back then they were not considered Aliens, legal or illegal, - they were just plain all-Americans like every other guy or gal that migrated to this country.

In those days Americans of Spanish ancestry (Mexicans) got to play all kinds of different parts in the movies. Remember the big epic movie "Ben Hur" starring Charlton Heston and a cast of thousands? Well, go back a little further to the silent movie era (1926) when MGM made the original movie of "Ben Hur."

This movie, also with a large cast, had Ramon Navarro (Mexican) play the part of "Ben Hur." Ramon Navarro, originally Ramon Samanyagos a Mexican dancer and movie extra, was discovered by Rex Ingram a talent scout in 1922. Mr. Ingram, who thought the name Samanyagos was too Mexican, changed it to "Navarro."

Ramon Navarro as "Ben Hur"

Ramon was a big movie star in his day. He was able to play just about any role they threw at him - Even if the part called for a non-Hispanic type. Unlike today's casting of Latinos, Ramon was called upon to play a variety of rolls from a sheik to an American business man. Rex Ingram also gave the starring role to Ramon in the mega-hit movie "The Prisoner of Zenda."

Lupe Velez

Another biggie of the early nineteen hundreds and of the Latin persuasion was a lovely lady by the name of "Lupe Velez." She was born Guadelupe Velez De Villabos in 1908 in Mexico. Raised in a convent in Texas, thirteen year old Lupe got her start in Mexico City as a dancer. Hollywood never heard of her until Hal Roach discovered her in 1926 and began to use her in two-reel comedies.

In 1927 Douglas Fairbanks cast Lupe as the heroine in the movie the "The Gaucho." Her role opposite Douglas Fairbanks, led to many more movie and stage opportunities. Miss Velez was hired by Florenz Ziegfeld to star in the musical "Hot Chah!" with Buddy Rogers.

Among her many musicals was "Strike me Pink" where she co-starred with Jimmy Durante. Like Ramon, she too was cast in various rolls. Before marrying Johnnie Weissmuller, she had a thing with Gary Cooper. She died in 1944 in her Beverly Hills home.

Remember Rita Moreno the Puerto Rican who starred in the classic musical "West Side Story" where she played one of the Puerto Rican gang girls. In the process of having makeup applied to her body, she asked the makeup artist "How come so much dark make up?" The artist's reply, "That's what she was told to do." Rita's response, "You know, there are light skinned Puerto Ricans too?"

Rita also starred in the movie "Four Seasons" about four couples who took regular vacations together. In an all white cast, she played an Italian married to a white guy. One interesting thing was her role called for her to repeat her ethnicity of Italian many times. Curiously, the ethnicity of the others was never a concern. Was it just too hard for an audience to accept a Latina married to a white guy?

Then there's the other Rita – "Rita Hayworth!"

Rita Hayworth (Age 16) with her father Eduardo Cansino

Most movie goers never realized that Rita was a Mexican from "Teejay." (Tijuana) In fact my boss, a product of the early black and white movies, wouldn't believe she was Hispanic until I showed him this picture of her dancing with her father.

She was first discovered dancing in a club in Tijuana. Unlike Rita Moreno, the fair skinned Rita Hayworth was a real American heartthrob who played mostly all non-Hispanic roles. (No need for dark makeup here)

There were other Hispanic stars of that era allowed to play multi-ethnic roles such as: Gilbert Roland, and Anthony Quinn. Despite their strong ethnic look, they too got to play a variety of roles. Some would say Anthony Quinn, besides having an Irish father, had quite an advantage by marrying Cecil B. DeMille's daughter.

But for certain reasons in some movie making, when a part called for a Mexican, they'd bypass talented available Hispanics and cast a white person to play the part. A few examples: Robbie Benson, Lou Diamond Phillips and Eli Wallach in his infamous role as the Mexican leader in the movie, "The Magnificent Seven."

And if it was an important Latino role that called for a big star, they'd use Jeffery Hunter. Yeah, the blond blue eyed white guy that played Jesus in "King of Kings." Contrary to my own beliefs, I thought Marlon Brando played a good Mexican in "Viva Zapata" - and Al Pachino really out did himself in the role as that legendary Puerto Rican "Scarface."

To Hollywood movie makers, along with most of Middle America, Mexicans are little brown people with limited abilities. They can only handle jobs requiring hard labor or something involving a menial task. In other words, they are not too bright! **And,** when the studios need a Mexican to play a Mexican, the actor is overly made up to appear the way real Americans believe Mexicans really look like. Just ask Rita Moreno!

But you know what? In this country, with the progress of blacks now playing the important roles, and Asians becoming so self-reliant, Mexicans are now called upon to fill the roles of maids, nannies, gardeners, and any other role that call for a subservient of sorts. I guess it's true! Art does imitate life. **Even President Nixon once said, "These brown people are built short for picking crops!"**

The American Indian and the Movies!

The American Indian, or Native American, or Redskin, or just plain ol' "Injun," other than "Iron Eyes Cody" and "Jay Silverheels," (Tonto) really didn't have much to do with the American cinema. In all those Cowboy and Indian movies, most of the Indians were really white guys with a lot of red make up. When they did use real Indians, all they had to know is how to fall off a horse and die.

Actor John Wayne and Director John Ford made a good living creating a poor image on the silver screen of the American Indian. Most of us Geezers were brought up on movies of good Cowboys and savage Indians. Kevin Costner kinda improved the image of the Native American when he made the movie "Dances with Wolves." He made them look almost human.

And again, the real juicy Indian parts were given to white actors. Remember Jeff Chandler as "Cochise" and Chuck Connors as "Geronimo?" And how about Tony Curtis playing the part of that World War II Indian hero, "Ira Hayes." Ira really wasn't a war hero. He just happened to be one of the guys that posed for the famous photo of the flag being raised on "Iwo Jima."

And typically, after the government and Hollywood got through exploiting Ira Hayes, he ended up just another drunken Indian – He died drunk and alone face down in a mud puddle. It has been pretty well established that alcoholism runs high among Native Americans.

Kids in the forties and fifties, by way of radio and movies, were regularly programmed to hate the native Indian and their barbaric ways. The following are examples of how the major studios portrayed the American Indian at such a low level of existence.

I remember an old movie called "Soldier of Fortune" staring Clark Gable and Susan Hayward. In the movie, which took place in China, a young adopted Chinese boy dressed like an American Cowboy told Clark he wanted to go to America and kill Indians. To defuse the boy's statement, Clark suggested that the boy pretend to be a spaceman. The boy's response was, "There are no Indians in space for me to kill." **Honest, this was the script - word for word!**

There were a lot of racist movies in those days. Most movies of that era were not concerned of what is now considered "politically correct." Here's another oldie but goodie that kinda helped us good Americans hate the dirty Injun.

In the movie "The Roaring Twenties" starring James Cagney, there's a scene where Cagney and a lady friend are seated in the living room when her six year old son enters the room. And again, we have the young boy dressed as an all American cowboy! When his mother asked him if he's been a good boy, his proud response was, "Yes Mommy, I just killed three Indians." The boy then turns to Cagney and asks, "Can you shoot a gun?" Cagney, who played a big time gangster in the movie, smiled at the boy and said, "Yes, but not lately." The boy then says to Cagney, "The next time you come over we can go out and kill Indians."

In those days racist dialog like this against any minority was not considered racist. Most of us, as kids, had no problem with dialog that pertained to the killing of wild Indians. AND, my father was part "Jacqui Indian!" Granted, although these movies were made 70 and 80 years ago, the pain to some is still real and painful. I guess we were so saturated with negative anti-Indian propaganda that no one really cared – Except, maybe the Indians.

Iron Eyes Cody – famous Native American Actor

I thought it appropriate to insert this famous photo of a teary eyed Iron Eyes Cody doing his commercial for environmental awareness.

Iron Eyes Cody, the dude with the real cool name, appeared in numerous movies – mostly westerns. He'll probably be remembered best for his environmental commercial, where he is shown sitting on his horse observing a polluted river with a tear in his eye.

Besides Iron Eyes, I can only recall one other Native American who became a famous movie star, Jay Silverheels. Jay, to me, is most famous for his portrayal of the Lone Ranger's sidekick "Tonto." I remember as a kid running home from school to listen to the Lone Ranger and Tonto. Along with making a few movies, they also had a TV series.

Speaking of the radio, TV, and the movies, I just thought of another famous sidekick - remember "Little Beaver?" who rode with "Red Ryder?" Unfortunately, they couldn't find a Native American kid so they got a white boy by the name of Robert Blake to play Little Beaver. I think Alan "Rocky" Lane played "Red Ryder."

I've always wondered how come the people who have been here the longest, and who at one time owned this place called America, really don't have too much to say about its function or direction. And these are people referred by all as Native Americans.

Anyway, thanks to Affirmative Action we now have a new batch of Native Americans starring and filling our TV's and silver screens with their acting abilities. Why there's ...…and ehhhh….and let's not forget eh…. - You know, come to think of it, Native Americans, really don't play much of a role in the entertainment business.

Part Ten

Minorities in

SPORTS

When it comes to racism and segregation in sports, the names Jim Thorp, Jessie Owens and Jackie Robinson come to mind.

Let's begin with Jim Thorp considered to be one of the greatest, if not the greatest, athlete to ever grace the athletic arenas. Jim Thorpe, one of the most accomplished all-around athletes in history, was selected in 1950 by American sportswriters and broadcasters as the greatest American athlete of the first half of the nineteenth century.

Jim was an American Indian of Sauk and Fox decent. His education included the Indian schools of Haskell in Kansas, and Carlisle Industrial School in Pennsylvania. While at Carlisle, Thorpe played football for coach Pop Warner. Because of his ability on the gridiron, Jim was picked as halfback for the all American teams of 1900 and 1912. Also in 1912, Thorpe competed in the decathlon and pentathlon in the Stockholm Olympics in which he won by a great margin.

Jim Thorpe – Carlisle half-back

Sadly to say in 1913 it was discovered by the Amateur Athletic Union that in 1909 and 1910, Jim had taken a summer job playing baseball for a little unknown baseball team. He did this out of necessity to help his family out financially. However, by Amateur Athletic Union standards, this put him in a professional bracket automatically disqualifying him from competing as an amateur. He subsequently had to give up his gold medals.

After losing his gold medals, and from 1913 to 1919, Jim went on to play professional baseball as an outfielder for the Boston Red Sox, the Cincinnati Reds, and the New York Yankees. Jim was unique in his natural ability as an athlete. Besides his ability with football and baseball, Jim excelled in such diverse sports as basketball – boxing – swimming – lacrosse - and hockey.

In his later years, despite his fame and notoriety as the greatest athlete of all time, his inability to adjust to a normal life was too much – And so to appease his discomfort with a life without sports he turned to the bottle which eventually led to his death. Sadly in 1982 after his death, Thorpe was subsequently restored as a winner of the decathlon and pentathlon of the 1912 Olympics. Even though Jim had won the competition by a great margin, he had to share the honors as a co-winner with the second place winners.

Next we have James (Jessie) Cleveland Owens (1913-1980) born in Danville, Alabama, one of the greatest track-and-field athletes of all time. He excelled in high school track, the running broad jump, the 100-yard dash, and the 200-yard dash. At Ohio State University, in 1935 & 36, he established two new world records; 26 ft, 8 ¼ inches in the running broad jump, and a new world record of 10.2 sec. for the 100-meter dash.

Jessie Owens – Track Star

As a member of the U.S. track team in the 1936 Olympics, held in Berlin, Jessie Owns won four gold medals. He won the 100-yard dash in 10.3 sec. equaling the Olympic record; set a new world record of 20.7 sec. in the 200-m dash; and won the running broad jump with a leap of 26 ft. 5 3/8 inches setting a new world record.

His fourth medal came as a member of the U.S. 400-m relay team that set a new Olympic and world record of 39.8 sec. Jessie did this in front of Adolph Hitler, the German leader and undisputed greatest White Supremacist that ever lived.

Despite Jessie's outstanding athletic performance, Hitler refused to acknowledge his Olympic victories because he was black. When the war with Germany and Japan came to an end, there was a serious push by government and all those concerned to put an end to segregation.

Blacks, who were not allowed to play in the all white major baseball league, created their own segregated Negro Leagues. The Kansas City Monarchs baseball team, a founding member of the National Negro League established in 1920, was considered to be one of the best. The Monarchs won the first Negro World Series title in 1924; then again won the series in 1924 and 1942.

The Kansas City Monarchs

Some of the greats that came out of that league were; Jackie Robinson, Hilton Smith, John "Buck" O'Neil, Ted Strong, Connie Johnson, Satchel Paige, and Pop Lloyd.

This segregation lasted until 1945 when Branch Rickey, General mangers of the Brooklyn Dodgers, realized segregation in major league baseball was not only politically indefensible but morally wrong. Mr. Rickey, concluding it would also bring in more fans and revenue, hired the first black man to ever play on a white team. History has proven Mr. Rickey made the right choice.

In 1945, Branch Rickey heard of a brilliant baseball player who happened to be playing for the Negro league by the name of Jackie Robinson. He signed this baseball phenom to play for the Dodgers Minor League Organization team in Montreal.

Jackie Robinson – Brooklyn Dodger

In Jackie's first year, his all around ability of hitting, fielding and running the bases, made him an instant star. Despite his athletic ability, Jackie is probably best known for being the first black man to break the color line in major league Baseball. And because of his special talent and ability, he kinda is responsible for integrated the major leagues by prompting other league team owners to hire blacks.

In less than ten years most teams had taken on black players. Jackie and Branch Rickey will always be known as main contributors in integrating major league baseball.

Back in the day, major league rosters were filled with the likes of Roy Campanella, Don Newcomb, Ernie Banks, Willey Mays, and Hank Aaron. The color of a player's skin was no longer a factor on the playing field - And in the stands fans, both black and white, sat side-by-side as they cheered for their favorite players - regardless of color.

How blacks were treated off the field was another thing entirely. These poor guys were treated miserably! They were continuously slapped in the face with racism as they traveled from city to city. They were separated from their white teammates by "Whites Only" signs in restaurants, hotels, and drinking fountains.

Anybody remember "Hammering Hank" and the ordeal he went through in 1972 when he attempted to break Babe Ruth's all time record of 714 homeruns? And how about the hate mail and death threats he received from hard working white middle-class Americans who resented this black guy out to break the "Great Bambinos" record? In 1973, Hank ended the season with 713 homeruns leaving him one homerun shy of Ruth's record.

This left him having to wait out the off-season until the 1974 season began before he could attempt to break Ruth's record. So during the long wait between seasons and the continued threats to his life, Hank and his family were placed under police protection - including his children in college.

Unfortunately for the European Americans, (white guys) African Americans (Black guys) are now quite prevalent on most baseball fields across the nation. As a matter of fact, they rank high on the roster of most sports.

The highest paid top three American athletes as of June 09 are considered black: Tiger Woods, Michael Jordan, and Kobe Bryant. (Updated news flash – as of October 2009, It was reported that Tiger woods became the first professional athlete in any sport to ever earn over a billion dollars.)

Hispanics, who have also been big money makers in all sports, have also had to deal with racism. Especially, those from the Islands! Being Hispanic is bad enough but being a black Hispanic - Forget it!
Take Roberto Walker Clememte for instance, the first Hispanic player elected to the Baseball Hall of Fame. Now this guy was not only a great ball player, but a great humanitarian.

Born in 1934 in Carolina, Puerto Rico, Roberto joined a professional baseball team at age seventeen. At seasons end in 1953, he was signed by the Brooklyn Dodgers. Because of his outstanding ability, Roberto in 1954 he was drafted by the last place Pittsburg Pirates.

Being a last place team, the Pirates welcomed Roberto's all around ability on the baseball field. With a batting average of 362, he led the pirates to two World Series championships – 1969 & 1971 – And in 1966 he was voted the National Leagues most valuable player – In that same year, his peers named him outstanding player of the year.
.

A friend of mine (A black guy) once asked me if Roberto Clemente was a Puerto Rican or a Blackman. I was surprised at his question. I in turn asked him if he considered himself to be a Black man or an American. This brought to light the standard argument that prevails in this country concerning race, color and nationality. Unlike the U.S.A. in other countries, color does not take preference over Nationality.

Since Jackie Robinson first opened the gate for all minorities to play Major league ball, the complexion of sports in all arenas and fields has changed from white to a greater mix of hues. Sadly though, this new mix of color is kinda confusing. Take for instance our next baseball super star, Alex Rodriguez.

Alex Rodriguez – New York Yankee star

Alex Rodriguez, a native New Yorker, considered by most to be the greatest baseball player ever, in 2008 was the highest paid athlete in baseball. With that said, and in this country, is Alex Rodriguez a Blackman, a Hispanic, a Dominican Republican American, or just a plain ol' "Mexican?"

The answer lies in the mind-sets and social levels of the white ruling class that programs...eh, I mean teaches us these things. Confusing isn't it? Because of Alex and Roberto's outstanding ability with a bat, they are claimed by all groups involved - Hispanics, Blacks, Dominicans, Puerto Ricans, and Americans.

Because of Alex Rodriguez's strong Hispanic name, the white media have chosen to give him a pet name they can live with – **"A-Rod."** Some other notable athletes considered to be of a multi-racial mix, whether the mix be Hispanic, Black, or Asian are: Tiger Woods, Derek Jeeter, Sammy Sousa, Orlando Zepeda, Tony Perez, etc.

Like the white population of this country, the Latino American society has a diverse mix of colors, cultures, and social levels. There are Hispanics like Keith Hernandez who kinda blend into society without too much fuss. Then we have Latinos who will never make the social level of Hispanic – they will always be noted as "Mexican!

Most Latino types, from places other than Mexico, are usually identified as Mexicans. And most of these faux Mexicans aren't too happy with their new label - unless it can find 'um a job. I wonder haw many times Alex Rodriguez, Roberto Clemente, and Sammy Sousa have been called Mexicans?

One popular guy everyone knew was a guy from Mexico named Fernando Valenzuela. He pitched for the Los Angeles Dodgers and **was a** natural phenomenon with a bigger than life presence creating the term "FERNANDOMANIA." Fernando drew crowds from all over. Everyone wanted to see him pitch. His most loyal and proudest fans were his countrymen from Mexico who traveled by any means possible – whether it be first class or burro.

Fernando Valenzuela – Los Angeles Dodger

Fernando himself came from humble beginnings - a small town in Mexico. After he became wealthy and popular, a sportscaster once asked him if he remembers when he was a poor kid in Mexico. Fernando's rapid response was, "I don't remember ever being poor."

Like most everything else in life, rich or poor is determined by your own evaluation. Fernando Valenzuela is one of those rare individuals fortunate enough to know where he's from and where he's going.

I discovered in researching these sports figures that some were listed in two categories – Like Roberto Clemente, and Alex Rodriguez who are listed in two different categories - African American and Hispanic. Then we have a guy like Tiger Woods, who's a mix of Black and Asian - A champion golf player everybody wants to claim.

Asians for some reason, other than tumbling (Gymnastics) and Ping- Pong (Table tennis), are never really considered athletic. These guys are too brainy to chase a ball of any size around a court or field. Maybe the attraction is the sound of all that money that is being tossed around.

And these Asian types are moving in on the All-American game of Baseball. Why, that's our game - I mean us Blacks and Hispanics! What will we do if the Asians take over baseball?

Take Hideo Nomo for instance, one of the first transplants from Japan to join the baseball ranks of America. He cashed in on all the big bucks by signing with the Los Angeles Dodgers - And as a Dodger, he became the first Japanese starting pitcher in the major leagues.

Hideo Nomo

Then there's "Ichiro Suzuki," the first ball player of any race to ever get 450 hits in his first two seasons.

I'm not a big fan of golf, but how 'bout those Asian women? In July 09, at the U.S. Open for women, I was surprised to see so many Asian women in contention. Five, were among the top ten finishers: South Korean "Eun Hee Ji" walked away with the big prize.

Eun Hee Ji – South Korean

Other great Asian athletes

BASKETBALL: We have Yao Ming who plays with the Houston Rockets. At first, because of his height, he was thought of as an awkward and clumsy oaf. The sports critics soon ate their words as they watched this 7 foot 6 inch lug gracefully move around the court.

FOOTBALL: Over on the gridiron, we have football linebacker Dat Nguyen of the Dallas Cowboys. Now this guy is living proof that Asians can mix it up with the so-called big and tough guys. I wonder who started that rumor anyway that Asians can only play sissy games like Ping-Pong and Tennis.

Hockey: Believe it or not, we have a Japanese Canadian by the name of Paul Kaiya who plays for the Anaheim Ducks. I'm not a hockey fan nor do I know anything about it, but one thing most of us would agree is that hockey is in no way a sissy game.

TENNIS: Michael Chang - The youngest male tennis player to win a grand slam (Age 17) Born in Hoboken, New Jersey, and because of his Asian ancestry, will always be known as a Chinese American. Chang was inducted into the International Tennis Hall of Fame.

Along with such great blacks as Arthur Ashe, we have the William sisters, Venus and Serena. These two girls, who are always in contention, ain't from no country club set either – they're from Watts in South Central Los Angeles.

Venus and Serena Williams

Venus and Serena with their superb talent with a racket have elevated the game of women's tennis to a new high.

The Williams sisters through out the years have competed against each other in the most prestigious courts in the world. In fact, in July 09, they competed for the coveted Wimbledon Cup. And after a hard and closely played game, Serena came away the winner.

Speaking of Watts - Remember Pancho Gonzales?

Ricardo Alonzo Gonzales – (Pancho) the other tennis champ from South Central Los Angeles is listed in the sports annuls as a Latino Legend - One of the great ones of yesteryear. Pancho, born in 1928, was inducted in the Hall of Fame in 1968.

As the complexion of sports continues to change we see more and more minorities getting on board the big money express. Because the number of whites has decreased in most major sports, especially in basketball, one disgruntled white guy has come up with an idea to solve this problem. He has introduced the concept of a whole new basketball league just for whites. Yeah, that should work!

As we come to the end of this chapter and the end of this book, I feel incomplete and unsatisfied knowing there is so much more I could write on minorities. I would've liked to have expounded more on minorities who are not really credited with being exceptional ethnic individuals and are hardly ever recognized as typical Americans contributing equally to society.

One thing I've learned in my seventy plus years of dealing with the white man boss is that they're not concerned so much that they'll find out you might be as good as they – they are more worried that **YOU** will find out that **"YOU"** are as good as they.

One white news guy, concerned with minorities rising to the top, put it best when he said, **"If the Minorities get our jobs - then what we will do?"**

And with that... this book is finished.

"DISGRUNTLED"
AIN'T SUCH A BAD THING!

It just means you're not satisfied with the status quo of the politics and business that affects the society you're involved in - And want to make a positive difference!

You won't compromise your personal ethics and go along with existing failing policies - nor do you want to turn your back on it and walk away. This is where you take on the new role of a **"Disgruntled Individual."**

More commonly known as a "Trouble Maker" or "Whistle Blower" - One willing to go against the grain regardless of the consequences.

Our history is filled with individuals disgruntled of existing situations: such as: Gandhi, Martin Luther King Jr. Mandela, Caesar Chavez, Rosa Parks, and last but not least – Jesus Christ. - All Disgruntled individuals not accepting the statue quo.